ESSENTIAL
BUDAPEST

★ Best places to see 34–55

Belváros and Lipótváros 115–136

■ Featured sight

Vár-hegy, Víziváros and Óbuda
75–104

Terézváros, Erzsébetváros and
Városliget 137–158

Gellért-I   áros
105–11

Original text by Rob Stuart

Revised and updated by Adrian Phillips and Monika Illés

© AA Media Limited 2012

First published 2008. Information revised and updated 2012

ISBN: 978-0-7495-7078-1

Published by AA Publishing, a trading name of AA Media Limited, whose registered office is Fanum House, Basing View, Basingstoke, Hampshire RG21 4EA. Registered number 06112600.

Colour separation: AA Digital Department

Printed and bound in Italy by Printer Trento S.r.l.

Find out more about AA Publishing and the wide range of services the AA provides by visiting our website at theAA.com/shop

A04463

Maps in this title produced from mapping © MAIRDUMONT/Falk Verlag 2011

Transport map ©Communicarta Ltd, UK

About this book

Symbols are used to denote the following categories:

- ✚ map reference to maps on cover
- ✉ address or location
- ☎ telephone number
- 🕐 opening times
- ✋ admission charge
- 🍴 restaurant or cafe on premises or nearby
- Ⓜ nearest underground train station
- 🚌 nearest bus/tram route
- 🚆 nearest overground train station
- ⛴ nearest ferry stop
- ✈ nearest airport
- ❓ other practical information
- ℹ tourist information office
- ► indicates the page where you will find a fuller description

This book is divided into six sections:

The essence of Budapest pages 6–19
Introduction; Features; Food and drink; Short break

Planning pages 20–33
Before you go; Getting there; Getting around; Being there

Best places to see pages 34–55
The unmissable highlights of any visit to Budapest

Best things to do pages 56–71
Great restaurants; stunning views; places to take the children and more

Exploring pages 72–169
The best places to visit in Budapest, organized by area

Excursions pages 170–183
Places to visit out of town

Maps
All map references are to the maps on the covers. For example, Országház has the reference ✚ 3F – indicating the grid square in which it is to be found

Admission Prices
Inexpensive (under 800Ft)
Moderate (800Ft–1,500Ft)
Expensive (over 1,500Ft)

Hotel prices
Prices for an en-suite double room with breakfast in high season:
€ inexpensive (under 25,000Ft)
€€ moderate (25,000–45,000Ft)
€€€ expensive (over 45,000Ft)

Restaurant prices
Two courses, per person, without drinks:
€ inexpensive (under 2,500Ft)
€€ moderate (2,500–5,500Ft)
€€€ expensive (over 5,500Ft)

Contents

THE ESSENCE OF...

6 – 19

PLANNING

20 – 33

BEST PLACES TO SEE

34 – 55

BEST THINGS TO DO

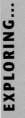

56 – 71

EXPLORING...

72 – 169

EXCURSIONS

170 – 183

The essence of...

Introduction   8–9

Features   10–11

Food and drink   12–15

Short break   16–19

Straddling the Danube with its nine bridges, Budapest has a bewildering array of architectural styles, a legacy of its turbulent history. Art nouveau, neoclassical, neo-Gothic and neo-Renaissance are just a few, and help create a skyline of astonishing grandeur. Budapest is not just a capital city, it is also a city of empire. Its sobriquet "Queen of the Danube" is rightly deserved. But make no mistake – far from being regally remote and austere, this queen is elegant, modishly cosmopolitan and inclined to drive in the fast lane.

features

If Europe has a centre, then it is Budapest. Hungary's capital not only straddles the Danube with ease and grace, but also the Continent's east-west divide. Here the two faces of Europe mingle, sometimes in harmony, at other times with unwanted friction. It is a place where the morning can be spent in the splendour of a royal palace and the afternoon hunting through a flea market for Russian cameras and GDR memorabilia. Or the entire day can be devoted to shopping for clothes, gorgeous antiques and authentic folk art. It doesn't really matter what you do, there's no escaping Budapest's unique charm.

It's no big surprise Budapest has a case of split personality though. On the west bank of the Danube is hilly Buda, the medieval heart of the city and favourite of the upper classes, and on the east is flat Pest (pronounced "pesht"), the commercial centre where the buzz of city life is loudest. Considering its history, the city should be psychotic! Ruled by the Turks for 150 years, dominated by the Habsburgs for generations, scarred by two world wars in the 20th century, then shrouded by the Soviet Iron Curtain for decades, and swamped by western consumerism in the last 20 years, Budapest has at times suffered terribly. Yet it has come through it all largely intact and with a tremendous energy.

Even on a short visit to Budapest, it's impossible not to be swept along by the city's vibrancy. And there is one thing Budapest will always provide: memorable experiences.

GEOGRAPHY

Hungary occupies the Carpathian Basin, a vast plain at the heart of East Central Europe. The River Danube divides Hungary's 93,030sq km (35,900sq miles) into the Great Plain (the Nagyalföld) on the east and Transdanubia (Dunántúl) on the west. The Great Plain is reminiscent of the Ukrainian steppes and the American prairie. Hungary's "mountains" are little more than hills, seldom exceeding 1,000m (3,280ft) in height. The highest peak is Kékes (1,014m/ 3,326ft) in the Mátra range northeast of Budapest. Much of Hungary is less than 200m (656ft) above sea level. Lake Balaton, southwest of Budapest, is the largest freshwater lake in Europe.

ECONOMY

Budapest is the commercial and industrial heart of Hungary. A burgeoning service sector, partly the result of booming tourism, is a major employer, though traditional manufacturing industries such as textiles, chemicals, iron and steel also employ a significant part of the population. With the advent of the free-market economy, Hungary has attracted substantial foreign investment, noticeably in the sectors of car assembly, high-tech electronics and light manufacturing.

LANGUAGE

Hungarian is a difficult language and a guess can lead to real confusion. German, which used to be the second language, has now been overtaken by English, especially among the young.

food & drink

Ask anyone to name a Hungarian dish and their answer invariably will be goulash. They will also make the mistake of calling it a "stew" when it is in fact a soup. Perhaps because of decades of communism, Central European cuisine has been associated with the sort of meal one would describe politely as filling, nutritious, yet unimaginative – a misconception. Although Hungarian cooking may struggle to compete with Europe's finest cuisine, its heartiness and unmistakable paprika flavours are enjoyed with gusto by anyone who has the privilege to sample it.

HUNGARIAN COOKING

Traditional Hungarian "peasant" cooking is based on the use of *rantas*, a rich roux of flour and pork lard. Bland and heavy, it requires lashings of paprika to spice it up. Paprika is still widely used and now thought of as a defining feature of Hungarian cooking. As the saying goes, "a real Magyar can handle his strong paprika well". Another characteristic is the use of sour cream, which adds a sharpness to the flavour. Soups and pasta

also figure strongly, with the ever-present paprika either on the table or already in the dish. Hungarian cuisine prides itself on being rich, full of flavour and substantial.

MEAT AND FISH

Most, if not all, Hungarian menus are dominated by meat dishes. Favourite meats are chicken, pork, veal, venison, duck and beef. Sometimes you can discover, as with "Tenderloin Steak Budapest Style", for instance, any number of different meats mixed together. In this case, the steak sits alongside smoked bacon, pork bones and goose livers (goose livers are a Hungarian speciality). Hence Hungarian cuisine's reputation for richness. River and lake fish are also well represented on Hungarian menus, especially pikeperch, carp and trout. As this is a landlocked country, the scarcity of sea fish is not surprising,

but if anyone can turn a pikeperch or carp (fish generally frowned upon elsewhere) into a mouthwatering dish, it's the Hungarians. A good fish soup is delicious, as is carp served with mushrooms in a tasty sour cream sauce.

VEGETARIANS

Vegetarians shouldn't entirely despair. These days most restaurants are sympathetic to dietary preferences and palates.

WINES, BEERS AND SPIRITS

You may be familiar with the legendary Egri Bikavér (Bull's Blood), which once rubbed corks on the lower shelves with popular *vins de table*. This wine is still very popular in Hungary, but for superior quality try Vesztergombi Bikavér from the Szekszárd region. Other good reds come from the vineyards in the Villány area to the southeast of Pécs. Etyek is a white-wine area just to the southwest of Budapest. White wines of quality are produced on the shores of Lake Balaton, the most interesting ones coming from the small vineyards in the lovely hilly country rising from the north shore. Tokaji is what Louis XIV of France called "the wine of kings, the king of wines". Rumour has it that since so little of this exceptional white wine is produced from that region, you're bound to buy a fake bottle. This is not true.

The best Hungarian beers are Kőbányai, Soproni and Dreher, but you'll also find an abundance of familiar foreign brands. Traditional Hungarian spirits are brandies called *pálinka*, and are available in various flavours such as cherry, plum and, most famously, apricot (*barackpálinka*). Be warned though: they are generally strong. Otherwise, all the usual spirits are available, for example whisky, vodka and gin. Those who prefer soft drinks can get anything from mineral water to cola.

short break

If you only have a short time to visit
Budapest, or would like to get a really
complete picture of the city, here are
the essentials:

● **Muse on, or be amused by,** Halászbástya
(Fishermen's Bastion), an architectural fantasy
that wouldn't look out of place on a Disney set
(➤ 40–41). There are wonderful views from its
top ramparts.

- **Visit Vörösmarty tér**, a broad pedestrianized square, but only after you've browsed the most exclusive shopping street, Váci utca (➤ 119).

- **Stand atop Gellért-hegy** (Gellért Hill) for spectacular views of the city, as well as the Citadella, a fortress built of white stone (➤ 38–39).

- **Marvel at the architectural** magnificence of Országház, the neo-Gothic Parliament building (➤ 48–49).

- **Wander the picturesque streets** of Vár-hegy (Castle Hill), or just soak up the atmosphere at one of the bars and cafes there (➤ 54–55).

- **Take a relaxing dip** in one of the many *gyógyfürdő* (thermal baths) if foot-sore from trudging the streets.

- **Stroll down Andrássy út**, once the most fashionable place to promenade in Budapest (➤ 138).

- **Take refuge from the hustle of the city** on peaceful Margitsziget (Margaret Island) in the middle of the Danube (➤ 44–45).

- **Visit the Budai Királyi Palota** (Buda Royal Palace) and the several museums in its confines (➤ 36–37).

- **Admire Mátyás-templom** (Matthias Church) in all its neo-Gothic magnificence in Szentháromság tér (Trinity Square, ➤ 46–47).

Planning

Before you go   22–25

Getting there   26–27

Getting around   28–29

Being there   30–33

Before you go

WHEN TO GO

JAN	FEB	MAR	APR	MAY	JUN	JUL	AUG	SEP	OCT	NOV	DEC
0°C	0°C	10°C	18°C	22°C	25°C	28°C	26°C	24°C	16°C	8°C	0°C
32°F	32°F	50°F	64°F	72°F	77°F	82°F	79°F	75°F	61°F	46°F	32°F

High season   Low season

(Temperatures are the average daily maximum for each month.)
Budapest is located in a temperate zone, and has a Continental climate characterized by cold winters (average temperature around 0°C/32°F), and hot summers (average daily maximum temperature 25°C/77°F), and a fair amount of rain in spring and autumn. Weather-wise, the best months to visit are May, June, September and October when temperatures are moderate, and clear, blue skies feature regularly as a city backdrop. That's not to say Budapest isn't gorgeous under a blanket of winter snow, but remember to bring a very warm coat. July and August can bring uncomfortably high temperatures.

Festivals are held throughout the year, but the largest concentration occur in spring and autumn (▶ 24–25).

WHAT YOU NEED

● Required
○ Suggested
▲ Not required

Some countries require a passport to remain valid for a minimum period (usually at least six months) beyond the date of entry – contact their consulate or embassy or your travel agent for details.

	UK	Germany	USA	Netherlands	Spain
Passport	●	●	●	●	●
Visa (regulations can change, check before your journey)	▲	▲	▲	▲	▲
Onward or Return Ticket	▲	▲	▲	▲	▲
Health Inoculations	▲	▲	▲	▲	▲
Health Documentation (▶ 23, Health Insurance)	●	●	●	●	●
Travel Insurance	○	○	○	○	○
Driving Licence (if driving; National or International)	●	●	●	●	●
Car Insurance Certificate (if own car)	●	●	●	●	●
Car registration document (if own car)	●	●	●	●	●

WEBSITES

- National Tourist Information Centre: www.tourinform.hu
- Budapest Tourist Office: www.budapestinfo.hu
- Hungarian Arts Festivals Federation: www.artsfestivals.hu
- Budapest Week: www.budapestweek.com

TOURIST OFFICES AT HOME

In the UK

Hungarian National Tourist Board
46 Eaton Place
London SW1X 8AL
☎ 020 7823 1032;
www.gotohungary.co.uk

In the USA

Hungarian Tourism Board
350 Fifth Avenue, Suite 7107
New York NY 10118
☎ 212/695-1221;
www.gotohungary.com

In Canada

Embassy of the Republic
of Hungary
302 Metcalfe Street
Ottawa, Ontario K2P 1S2
☎ (613) 230-2717

In Australia

Consulate General of Hungary
Suite 405, 203–233 New South
Head Road, Edgecliff, NSW 2027
☎ (02) 9328 7859;
www.hunconsydney.com

HEALTH INSURANCE

All visitors receive free first aid and transport to hospital. Citizens of EU countries receive free further treatment (if they have a European Health Insurance Card), but comprehensive health insurance is recommended. Non-EU citizens should make sure they have full health cover.

TIME DIFFERENCES

| GMT
12 noon | → Budapest
1PM | → Germany
1PM | ← USA (NY)
7AM | → Netherlands
1PM | → Spain
1PM |

Hungary is on Central European Time, one hour ahead of Greenwich Mean Time (GMT+1), but from late March to late October, daylight saving (GMT+2) operates.

NATIONAL HOLIDAYS

1 Jan *New Year's Day*

15 Mar *Anniversary of 1848–49 Revolution*

Mar/Apr *Easter Monday*

1 May *Labour Day*

May/Jun *Whit Monday*

20 Aug *St Stephen's Day*

23 Oct *Anniversary of 1956 Revolution*

1 Nov *All Saints' Day*

25 Dec *Christmas Day*

26 Dec *Boxing Day*

In Hungary most offices, shops and other facilities close down on public holidays and, should any of these holidays be on a Tuesday or Thursday, the day between it and the weekend also becomes a public holiday.

WHAT'S ON WHEN

March *Budapest Spring Festival:* A fortnight of first-class concerts, opera, dance, theatre and folklore performances, as well as master classes and exhibitions at several venues in the city.

April *National Dance House Meeting and Fair,* Budapest Sports Arena: A whirl of music and dance lessons, amateur and professional performances, folk artists and handicraft displays.

June *Week of Books:* A celebration of Hungarian literature, with interviews, performances and publishing-house stalls around the city centre.

Wine Festival, Városliget: A gastronomic festival in the City Park featuring top wines and winemakers, gypsy and folk music, and a lively market atmosphere.

Bridge Festival: A carnival marks the anniversary of the Széchenyi Lánchíd (Chain Bridge) with festivities taking place on and around the bridge.

Budapest Fair, Hősök tere: This summer carnival commemorates the withdrawal of Soviet troops from Hungary. It features jazz and classical music, street theatre and children's entertainment.

July *Summer on the Chain Bridge:* Each weekend from July to mid-August, the city's oldest bridge is taken over by pedestrians, with free music concerts, performances and other entertainment taking place.

Budafest Summer Music Festival: Opera, ballet and jazz in the Hilton Hotel's Dominican Courtyard, symphony orchestras outside St Stephen's Basilica, and opera and ballet at the Opera House (► 42–43).

August *Sziget Festival:* A week-long Hungarian "Woodstock", with top international bands attracting around 400,000 visitors to Óbuda Island.

St Stephen's Day: Countrywide celebrations, processions and fireworks.

Budapest Parade: Carnival floats parade along Andrássy út, with parties starting up in the Stadium Gardens after 10pm.

Jewish Summer Festival, Jewish district: A week celebrating Jewish culture, with books, films, gastronomy, music and dance in the Jewish district (late August to early September).

September *Budafok Wine Festival,* Budafok Cellars: Cellar tours, wine-tasting, concerts, music and dance.

International Wine Fair, Buda Royal Palace: Cultural programme and grape-harvest procession.

SzeptemberFeszt: A three-day gastronomic festival with various cooking competitions, music and children's entertainment.

October *Budapest Autumn Festival:* A ten-day contemporary arts festival focusing on new directions in music, theatre, dance, art, film and literature.

December *Budapest Christmas,* Vörösmarty tér: Arts and crafts are sold in the city centre alongside steaming vats of mulled wine.

New Year's Eve Gala and Ball, Opera House: A gala concert in the beautiful Opera House, with a festive supper prepared by chefs from Gundel restaurant, followed by a New Year's Ball until dawn.

Getting there

BY AIR

Budapest, Ferihegy Airport,

20km (12 miles) to city centre

🚃 25 minutes (Terminal 1 to Nyugati)

🚐 Minibus 30 minutes

🚗 30 minutes

Budapest's Ferihegy Airport (tel: 296 7000, www.bud.hu) receives flights from across the globe. Hungary's national airline, Malév (tel: 06 40 212 12, www.malev.hu), has direct flights to and from North America and much of Europe, including the UK and Ireland. There are several ways to reach the city centre from the airport. The Airport Shuttle Minibus will drop you anywhere in Budapest; it costs 2,990Ft one-way and 4,990Ft return. If there are more than two passengers, it's cheaper by taxi. Főtaxi, the official airport company, offers set prices from 5,100Ft to 5,700Ft, depending on where you are going to. There are kiosks for Főtaxi and the minibus in the arrivals hall. A fast train service runs between Terminal 1 and Budapest Nyugati station. The journey takes around 25 minutes and costs 365Ft one way. You can take buses 93 (from Terminal 1 only) and 200/200E (from either terminal) to the Kőbánya-Kispest terminus (from where you can take the blue M3 Metro line to the centre).

BY RAIL

Budapest is linked to Europe's comprehensive rail network by Magyar Államvasutak (www.mav.hu), Hungary's state railway. International trains call at one of the city's three main stations:
Keleti (east) ✉ Kerepesi út 2–4, Budapest VII ☎ 06 40 49 49 49;
Déli (south) ✉ Krisztina körút 37, Budapest I ☎ 06 40 49 49 49;
Nyugati (west) ✉ Teréz körút 55, Budapest VI ☎ 06 40 49 49 49.

BY CAR

The M1 links Budapest with Vienna, the M7 heads southwest to Croatia via Lake Balaton, the M5 travels south towards Serbia, and the M3 leads east as far as the city of Nyíregyháza.

BY BUS

Eurolines (www.eurolines.com) buses travel from London and many points on the Continent to Budapest, arriving at Népliget bus station (Üllői út 131, Budapest IX, tel: 219 8063) in Pest.

BY BOAT

Ferries and hydrofoils travel between Vienna and Budapest on the Danube from April to October. They dock at the Nemzetközi hajóállomás (International Ferry Pier, Belgrád rakpart, Budapest V), which is located in Pest between Erzsébet híd and Szabadság híd. For more information on these ferry and hydrofoil services see www.mahartpassnave.hu or www.ddsg-blue-danube.at.

Getting around

PUBLIC TRANSPORT

Metro As well as the below-street and rather charming M1 or *földalatti* ("underground"), which has linked central Pest with Heroes' Square since 1896, there are two deep Metro lines, M2 (red) and M3 (blue). These connect the city centre with the main railway stations and some of the suburbs.

Buses Around 200 bus and 15 trolleybus routes fill in the gaps between the tram and the Metro network in Budapest. One of the easiest ways of getting up Castle Hill is to take the dinky Várbusz (castle bus) from Moszkva tér.

River boats The scheduled passenger service operating on the Danube (May–Aug daily 8–6) is an excellent and inexpensive way of seeing the city from a fresh angle.

Trams These connect many important tourist destinations and can be an excellent way of sightseeing (outside rush hours). Especially useful routes include 2 along the Pest bank of the Danube, and 4 and 6 along the Outer Ring to Moszkva tér interchange, where they link with the Várbusz.

HÉV surburban trains These connect Budapest with outlying suburbs and towns. The most useful are the ones to Szentendre (leaving from Batthyány tér) and Gödöllő (from Örs vezér tere).

Fares and tickets Tickets must be bought before boarding public transport and can be purchased at Metro stations, some tram stops and news-stands. Validate tickets at Metro entrances and on trams, trains and buses. Note that ticket controls are a regular occurrence – the fine is 6,000Ft, to be paid on the spot or at a BKV office (Budapest Transport Company, www.bkv.hu). Children up to the age of six travel free with an adult, and there is no charge either for EU citizens over 65 (ensure you have a passport or other recognized ID as proof of age). A single ticket costs 320Ft and is valid on the same Metro train, tram, bus or trolleybus as long as you do not change lines or backtrack. A block of 10 tickets is available for 2,800Ft. Transfer tickets (490Ft) allow one line change within 1.5 hours. Tickets covering Metro travel only are also available; a section ticket costs 260Ft and is valid for three stops within 30 minutes. The simplest solution is a one-day ticket *(napijegy,* 1,550Ft), three-day tourist ticket *(72 órás jegy,* 3,850Ft), or seven-day travelcard *(hetijegy,* 4,600Ft). Each allows unlimited travel on all forms of BKV transport (except ferries). Fortnightly (6,500Ft) and monthly (9,800Ft) passes are also available but a photo is required to purchase them.

TAXIS

Taxi companies include:
Budataxi ☎ 233 3333; Citytaxi ☎ 211 1111; Főtaxi ☎ 222 2222; Rádiotaxi ☎ 777 7777; Tele5 ☎ 555 5555; 6x6Taxi ☎ 666 6666. Be careful of rogue taxis that do not display signs.

DRIVING

- Speed limit on motorways (highways): 130kph (80mph)
- Speed limit on major roads: 100kph (60mph). Other roads: 90kph (56mph). Cars with trailers/coaches: 70kph (43mph)
- Speed limit in built-up areas: 50kph (30mph)
- Seat belts must be worn in front seats and rear seats where fitted.
- There is a total alcohol ban for drivers in Hungary.
- Petrol is readily available. Opening times vary, but there are 24-hour stations.
- Self-service is the norm at petrol stations. Credit cards are not accepted everywhere.
- You can contact the Hungarian Automobile Club by calling 212 2821 or 118 (24-hour service). In the case of an accident call the police (tel: 107 or 112) immediately.
- Vehicles with damaged bodywork may leave the country only if they have an official certificate.

CAR RENTAL

There are many car-rental firms operating in Hungary, including Avis, Hertz and Fox Autorent. The driver must be over 21 and have held a licence for more than one year.

Being there

TOURIST OFFICES
National Tourist Information Centre (Tourinform)
- Sütő utca 2, Budapest V
  (near Deák tér Metro station)
  ☎ 438 8080;
  www.tourinform.hu

Touchscreen Information
- Tourinform offices
- Ferihegy Airport
- Déli railway station

- Liszt Ferenc tér 11,
  Budapest VI ☎ 322 4098
Tourism Office of Budapest
- Nyugati railway station
  Teréz körút 55, Budapest VI
  Main Concourse ☎ 302 8580

- Astoria Metro station
- Grand Market Hall

MONEY
The monetary unit of Hungary is the forint (HUF), abbreviated to Ft. Coins are in denominations of 10, 20, 50, 100 and 200 forints. Most purchases involve the use of banknotes, which come in denominations of 200, 500, 1,000, 2,000, 5,000, 10,000 and 20,000 forints.

Traveller's cheques and convertible currency can be changed in banks, travel offices and hotels, and credit cards are in increasing use, although they are not accepted everywhere. Eurocheques may be used up to a limit of 30,000Ft. ATMs are widely available. Check with your card provider that you can use your card abroad and ask about the charges.

TIPS/GRATUITIES

Yes ✓   No ✗

Hotels (if service not included)	✓	10%
Restaurants (if service not included)	✓	10–20%
Cafes/bars	✓	10%
Taxis	✓	10%
Hairdressers	✓	10–15%
Usherettes	✓	change
Cloakroom attendants	✓	change
Toilets	✓	change
Garage attendants	✓	change

POSTAL AND INTERNET SERVICES

The city's main post office is at Petőfi Sándor utca 13–15, Budapest V, (Mon–Fri 8–8, Sat 8–2). Nyugati train station post office is at Teréz körút 51, Budapest VI (Mon–Fri 7am–8pm, Sat 8–6).

Budapest is dotted with internet cafes and all shopping malls contain one. A number of bars, restaurants and cafes provide WiFi free of charge.

TELEPHONES

Public telephones are widely available. Most accept phonecards rather than coins. Phonecards can be bought at hotels, newsagents, petrol stations, tobacconists and post offices.

For local calls, dial the number required. For national calls dial 06, the area code and number. You must also dial 06 when calling mobile phones. For international calls, dial 00, the country access code, the area code (minus any initial "0") and the number. The country code to call Hungary from abroad is 36, followed by 1 for Budapest numbers.

International dialling codes

From Hungary to:

UK: 00 44

Germany: 00 49

USA and Canada: 00 1

Netherlands: 00 31

Spain: 00 34

Emergency telephone numbers

Police: 107

Fire: 105

Ambulance: 104

General emergency number: 112

EMBASSIES AND CONSULATES

UK ☎ 266 2888

Germany ☎ 488 3500

USA ☎ 475 4400

Netherlands ☎ 336 6300

Spain ☎ 202 4006

HEALTH ADVICE

Sun advice During summer temperatures can rise above 30°C (85°F), with bright sunshine. Wear a sunhat and cover your skin as Budapest can receive around nine hours of sunshine per day in July and August.

Drugs Pharmacies (*gyógyszertár* or *patika*) issue a wide range of drugs. Take special medication you need with you.

Safe water Tap water is safe to drink. Bottled water is widely available. Look for *ásványvíz* (mineral water) or *szénsavas ásványvíz* (sparkling water).

PERSONAL SAFETY

Security in Budapest is no worse than in any other European capital city. The most frequent crimes are pickpocketing, confidence tricks and car theft. Tourist Police and uniformed guards, accompanied by interpreters, patrol main tourist areas from July to August.

- Avoid street vendors and beggars.
- Beware of attractive offers.
- Don't carry too much cash.
- Never leave valuables in your car.

Victims of crime should contact the English-language crime hotline (24 hours) ☎ 438 8080.

ELECTRICITY

The power supply in Budapest is 220 volts AC. Sockets accept two-pin round plugs, so an adaptor is needed for most non-Continental European appliances, and a transformer is required for appliances operating on 100–120 volts.

OPENING HOURS

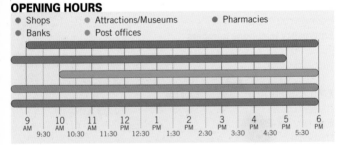

Shops close early on Saturday afternoons – few remain open after 1pm. They open late (7–8pm) on Thursdays. Supermarkets and other food shops have longer hours and are open on Sunday mornings. Shops in malls and in areas frequented by tourists also have longer hours and are open on Sundays. Pharmacies follow shop hours but there is always one open late in each area. Banks close early (1pm) on Fridays.

The majority of museums are closed on Monday; in winter they usually close earlier. Large churches are open throughout the day, in small towns and villages they may open only early morning and/or evening (6–9pm).

LANGUAGE

Hungarian (Magyar) belongs to the Finno-Ugric group and lies outside the mainstream of European languages. While its spellings are logical, understanding and speaking it pose considerable difficulties to foreigners. Guesswork and improvisation can lead to considerable confusion. English has replaced German as the principal second language, especially among the young. Locals in service industries usually speak English, and hotel staff may understand several languages.

Do you speak English?	*Beszél angolul?*	good morning/ night	*jó regggelt/éjszakát*
I don't understand	*Nem értem*	goodbye	*viszontlátásra*
yes	*igen*	please	*kérem*
no/not	*nem*	thank you	*köszönöm*
hotel	*szálloda*	per person/per room	*egy személyre/*
room	*szoba*		*egy szoba ára*
single/double	*egyágyas/ francia ágyas*	reservation	*foglalás*
		rate	*szobaár*
one/two nights	*egy/kettő éjszakára*	breakfast	*reggeli*
bank	*bank*	foreign exchange	*külföldi deviza*
exchange office	*pénzváltó*	foreign currency	*külföldi valuta*
post office	*posta*	pound sterling	*font*
cashier	*pénztáros*	US dollar	*dollár*
restaurant	*étterem*	wine list	*borlista*
cafe	*kávéház*	lunch	*ebéd*
table	*asztal*	dinner	*vacsora*
menu	*menükartya*	starter	*előétel*
set menu	*menu*	main course	*főétel*
aeroplane	*repülőgép*	ferry terminal	*komp kikötő*
airport	*repülőtér*	ticket	*jegy*
train	*vonat*	single/return	*egyirányú/retúr*
station	*állomás*	first/second class	*első/másodosztályú*
bus station	*buszallomás*	ticket office	*jegypénztár*

Best places to see

Budai Királyi Palota
(Buda Royal Palace)   36–37

Gellért-hegy (Gellért Hill)   38–39

Halászbástya (Fishermen's Bastion)   40–41

Magyar Állami Operaház
(Hungarian State Opera House)   42–43

Margitsziget (Margaret Island)   44–45

Mátyás-templom (Matthias Church)   46–47

Országház (Parliament)   48–49

Szent István Bazilika
(St Stephen's Basilica)   50–51

Szépművészeti Múzeum
(Fine Arts Museum)   52–53

Vár-hegy (Castle Hill)   54–55

1 Budai Királyi Palota (Buda Royal Palace)

By far the most grandiose building in Buda, ironically this is a palace whose royals have never been resident, only visiting guests.

No other building in Buda reflects so dramatically the turbulent history of the Castle District. Built in the second half of the 13th century by King Béla IV, after the invasion of the Mongols, centuries of war, invasion and revolution have left little of the palace's original architecture. Razed to the ground during World War II, it was later rebuilt in baroque style. A magnificent stairway leads to the entrance of the palace proper, where the steep east wall widens into the deep embrasure. Note the statue of Prince Eugene of Savoy, leader of the military operations that forced the Turks finally to retreat.

The double middle wing of the palace, including the dome, houses the National Gallery (➤ 79), with its comprehensive collection of Hungarian painting and sculpture. To reach the other museums, walk through the narrow passage to the west side through a pretty garden square, where you will see the Matthias Well (depicting King Matthias in a hunting scene), regarded as one of the most beautiful fountains in Budapest (➤ 79–80). The west wing houses the National Széchényi

Library (▶ 80), with its vast collection of about 10 million works in the form of books, manuscripts, magazines and periodicals.

At the south end of the courtyard is the entrance to the Budapest History Museum (▶ 78), where 2,000 years of the city's history are presented, including the marvellous Renaissance stone collection, which illustrates the former lavishness of the Palace of Matthias Corvinus.

Facing the museum's entrance is a glass door beyond which lies a steep flight of stairs. All that remains, or was possible to recover and reconstruct, of the medieval royal castle and fortress can be seen in the basement. You may by now feel inclined to spend a little time in the Hűsölo (cooling-off chamber) situated under the Great Hall – these are cellars where the king's courtiers came to get out of the hot sun.

In the grounds of the royal palace, and worth a closer look in themselves, are the lions that guard the entrance of Oroszlános udvar (The Lion Courtyard), designed by János Fadrusz in 1904. With their grim looks, two of these stone animals seem intent on discouraging visitors. Those brave enough to enter the lions' den are then met by two more inside the gate, roaring angrily. The huge door in the gateway between the lions leads to an elevator that takes you down to the bottom of the wing overlooking Buda.

➕ 3J ✉ Szent György tér, Budapest 1 🕐 Open access to the grounds throughout the year. Museums: Tue–Sun 10–6 ✋ Museums: inexpensive–moderate 🍴 Rivalda (€€€, ▶ 100) 🚌 Bus: 16, Várbusz. Funicular from Clark Ádám tér

2 Gellért-hegy (Gellért Hill)

Rising to a height of 230m (755ft) between Erzsébet (Elizabeth) and Szabadság (Liberty) bridges over the Danube, this is perhaps the best vantage point from which to see Budapest.

Named after Bishop Gellért (Gerard), who was given the unenviable task of converting the reluctant Magyars to Christianity, this hill provides a commanding view of Budapest, and overlooks Elizabeth Bridge, from which, according to legend, the bishop was cast into the Danube by a bunch of stubborn heathens.

At the foot of the hill are the Rudas Gyógyfürdő (Rudas baths, ➤ 110), with their unmistakable domed roof, and inside, an octagonal pool. Crowning the hill is the Citadella (➤ 106), a white stone fortress built to restore order in the aftermath of the 1848–49 War of Independence. Today, as a restaurant, hotel and wax museum, it fortifies nothing more than the hungry and foot-weary.

The hill is crowned by the Szabadság szobor (Liberation Monument, ➤ 109), a striking statue of a woman holding a palm branch aloft. It was raised by the Russians in 1947 and originally incorporated a Soviet soldier, complete with red flag – tactfully removed after the collapse of communism to the Szoborpark (Memento Park, ➤ 175).

Towards Liberty Bridge you can see the Gellért Hotel (➤ 107), once the HQ of the authoritarian regent Admiral Horthy. Now the houses and apartments of the well-heeled dominate this area.

✚ 4L ✉ Budapest I, XI ❸ Open access ⚑ Citadel: inexpensive ⑪ Restaurant (€€) 🚌 Bus: 27. Tram: 18, 19, 47, 49

3 Halászbástya (Fishermen's Bastion)

Wrapping around a magnificent statue of King Stephen mounted on his steed, the Fishermen's Bastion is a turreted, Disneyesque edifice on the eastern edge of Castle Hill.

The Halászbástya, named after the fishermen's guild that defended the area in the Middle Ages, is one of Budapest's most eccentric structures. Affectedly Gothic in style, it owes more, perhaps, to the precocious imagination of its Hungarian architect, Frigyes Schulek, than to any serious architectural tradition.

Its seven conical towers represent the tents of the seven Magyar tribes who followed King Árpád into modern-day Hungary in the ninth century AD, founding the Magyar kingdom.

The bastion was built as a viewing platform in 1905 during renovations to Mátyás-templom (Matthias Church, ➤ 46–47) and its surrounds. It was one of several large-scale municipal building and renovation projects instigated to celebrate the 1,000th anniversary of the arrival of the ancestors of today's Hungarians. It provides a wonderful view from its top ramparts, which takes in Pest, the Danube, beautiful Margitsziget (Margaret Island, ➤ 44–45) and the city's string of bridges. Looking over to Pest, Szent István Bazilika (St Stephen's Basilica, ➤ 50–51) demands the attention of any viewer, but it is the magnificent Országház (Parliament, ➤ 48–49), with its huge central dome, that steals the architectural show.

Nearby in the Budai Királyi Palota (Buda Royal Palace, ➤ 36) is the Magyar Nemzeti Galéria (Hungarian National Gallery, ➤ 79), filled with magnificent Hungarian cultural artefacts, including altarpieces, wood panels, paintings dating from the 13th to the 16th centuries, and works by modern and contemporary artists. It's an edifying contrast to the architectural absurdity of the bastion.

✚ 2H ✉ Szentháromság tér, Budapest I ⊙ Open access
👆 Free. Upper arcade: inexpensive ❚❚ Ruszwurm (€, ➤ 102)
🚌 Bus: 16, Várbusz. Funicular

4 Magyar Állami Operaház (Hungarian State Opera House)

www.opera.hu

Among the most beautiful opera houses in Europe, the opulence of this building may distract you from the performance.

Commissioned by the Emperor Franz Joseph, the State Opera House was begun in 1875 under the close supervision of architect Miklós Ybl, who apparently checked every cartload of stone. Italian-Renaissance in style, its interior is voluptuously marbled, gilded and decorated with frescoes by some of the finest painters of the time. It opened in 1884 and attracted the biggest names in opera. Gustav Mahler was music director for a time, and after World War II Otto Klemperer took up the directorship. On the stone cornice of the terrace are statues of composers including Mozart, Verdi, Wagner and Beethoven; but niches by the main entrance are reserved for the great 19th-century Hungarian composers Erkel and Liszt. Above the vast auditorium, seating 1,289 people, a three-tonne bronze chandelier hangs from a ceiling decorated with a fine fresco by Károly Lotz.

Despite its *fin de siècle* atmosphere, it is an entirely "modern" building with all-metal hydraulic stage machinery, an iron curtain and even a sprinkler system. After renovations, the opera house reopened in all its magnificence in 1984, exactly 100 years after the first performance here.

This building is a real treat, and likely to be a highlight of your itinerary. Tickets for performances are available from the box office, but beware: not all seats in the auditorium offer views of the stage.

➕ 5G ✉ Andrássy út 22, Budapest VI ☎ 332 7914. Box office: 353 0170 🕐 Guided tours: Mon–Sun 3 and 4. Box office: Mon–Sat 11–7, Sun 4–7. Performances: regular but not daily 💶 Guided tour: expensive 🍴 Belcanto (€€, ➤ 152) 🚇 M1 Opera 🚌 Bus: 105

5 Margitsziget (Margaret Island)

Adrift in the Danube, this idyllic island is the perfect escape from the hustle and bustle of the city.

Citizens of Budapest will claim, quite justifiably, that Margaret Island in the Danube is one of Europe's first parks. While not large by city park standards – its length can be strolled in about an hour – it's worth allowing plenty of time for leisurely exploration. It was originally three islands, and the Romans built the first bridge to connect them with the Buda shore. The largest island was called Rabbit Island, reflecting its status as a royal hunting reserve. Its present name was given in honour of King Béla's daughter Margit, who retired to a nunnery there in 1252, at the age of nine. During the Turkish occupation it was home to a harem.

Credit must go to the Habsburg gardeners who planted many of the 10,000 trees, most of them plane trees. Here, but under an oak, poet János Arany (1817–82) composed "Under the Oak Trees".

There are various amenities on the island, including swimming pools, a theatre, zoo, rose garden and Japanese garden, as well as a plethora of statues. You can hire bikes and fun pedal cars. At the northern end is the famous old Grand Hotel (now the Danubius Grand Hotel Margitsziget), whose terrace is a pleasant place on which to relax and enjoy the tranquil atmosphere.

✚ 4B ✉ River Danube – between Árpád and Margaret bridges, Budapest XIII ⏰ Open access 🖐 Free
🍴 Danubius Grand Hotel Margitsziget (€€€, ➤ 96)
🚌 Bus: 26. Tram 4, 6 ❓ Access by car from Árpád Bridge and then only as far as the car park next to the Grand Hotel Margitsziget, otherwise cars prohibited on the island

6 Mátyás-templom (Matthias Church)

www.matyas-templom.hu

Some claim this as a masterpiece of European eclecticism; others compare it to over-decorated stage scenery. It's certainly a bold piece of architectural design.

Originally the place of worship of the German burghers, and dedicated to the Blessed Virgin in Buda, the church owes its popular name to the fact that the legendary Hungarian king Mátyás (Matthias Corvinus, 1458–90) held both his weddings here. Parts date from the 13th century, but the main body of the church was extensively rebuilt in the 19th century. The dazzling, but muted, interior – the result of extensive restoration work carried out by Frigyes Schulek between 1874 and 1896 – recalls many of the original medieval designs. Note the beautiful floral motifs and geometric patterns on the walls. The Turks turned the building into a mosque, and later it was converted into a baroque church. Schulek's dream was to restore it to as much of its original condition as possible, though his enthusiasm for the ornate is all too evident, especially in the spectacular 80m-high (262ft) spire.

Enter the church through the Mary Portal, where you can see a 14th-century relief depicting the death of the Virgin. In the Loreto Chapel, to the left of the Mary Portal, is a Gothic triptych and a baroque black Madonna dating from 1700. By the main altar hangs the original coat of arms of Matthias Corvinus ("The Raven", ➤ 80). Two chapels, one dedicated to St Imre (son of St Stephen, the first Christian king of Hungary); the other, the Trinity Chapel, housing the tombs of 12th-century king Béla III and his wife, Anne of Châtillon, are to be found near the main door. Do not miss the impressive collection of ecclesiastical art in the two oratories.

➕ 2H ✉ Szentháromság tér 2, Budapest I ☎ 355 5657
🕐 Mon–Fri 9–5, Sat 9–12:15, 1:45–4:30, Sun 1–5
✋ Moderate; includes collection of ecclesiastical art
🍴 Ruszwurm (€, ➤ 102) 🚌 Bus: 16, Várbusz. Funicular

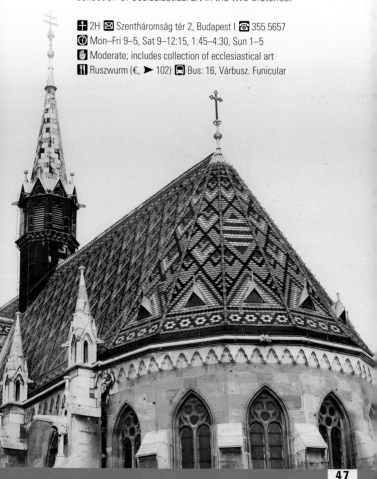

7 Országház (Parliament)

www.parlament.hu

Budapest's magnificent Parliament building is a vivid expression of Hungarian national identity.

A glorious neo-Gothic edifice with many towers and pinnacles, the building was started in 1885, and completed in 1902. Today it remains a symbol of pride in the independent kingdom, and a testament to the wealth of Hungary's industrial age.

The huge central dome is 96m (315ft) high – a deliberate reference to the Magyar conquest of Hungary in AD896. It dominates a structure that encompasses ten courtyards and 691 rooms. Beneath the dome is a grand 16-sided hall, flanked to the north and south by chambers for the two houses of the Hungarian Parliament (now a single National Assembly).

Statues occupy the central hall (a bust of the Parliament's architect, Imre Steidl, stands modestly off the main staircase), which is still used for state occasions. Additional statues of rulers and military leaders adorn the outside of the building.

Not everyone admires the building, but for many it is the most outstanding example of neo-Gothic architecture on a grand scale in the whole of Europe. Tours of the Parliament pass through the Congress Hall, the main staircase and the Domed Hall, where the country's most valuable item, Szent István's crown, is displayed alongside other precious objects.

➕ 3F ✉ Kossuth Lajos tér 1–3, Budapest V ☎ Tours: 441 4904 🕐 Guided tours (in English): daily 10, 12, 2; curtailed during parliamentary sessions 🎟 Free (EU citizens); expensive (non-EU citizens) 🍴 Iguana Bar and Grill (€€), Zoltan utca 16 🚇 M2 Kossuth Lajos tér 🚌 Bus: 15. Tram: 2. Trolleybus: 70, 78

8 Szent István Bazilika (St Stephen's Basilica)

www.basilica.hu

The vicissitudes of its construction might well have tested even the patience of God himself, for this basilica took 55 years to build.

This huge church, the largest in the city, holds 8,500 people. Work started in 1851 but it wasn't completed until 1905. The ground plan of the basilica represents the shape of a Greek cross, and is divided into nine barrel-vaulted parts, with a cupola in the middle. No expense was spared: 41kg (90lb) of 24-carat gold were used for the gilding, while 88 statues adorn the exterior, celebrating, on the Danube side, the Hungarian rulers, and on the Kossuth side, the princes of Transylvania and several famous commanders.

The interior is ornamented with paintings, tapestries, sculptures and frescoes by major Hungarian artists: Mór Thán, Bertalan Székely, Gyula Benczúr, Károly Lotz, Alajos Stróbl, János Fadrusz, Pal Pátzay and Beni Ferenczy.

St Stephen is the country's patron saint. Crowned king of Hungary in 1000, it was Stephen who accepted Christianity, thus bringing his country into the community of Europe. The *Szent Jobb*, his mummified right hand, is

preserved in a richly
ornamented glass case in
one of the chapels. It is
the Hungarian Roman
Catholic Church's most
revered relic, carried
in procession every
St Stephen's Day
(20 August).

Many important
documents and art
treasures were stored
in the cellars for their
protection during the
siege of Budapest in
early 1945. A restoration
programme has returned
the building to its original
pristine appearance. Climb
to the dome for fine views.

✚ 5H ✉ Szent István tér,
Budapest V ☎ 338 2151
🕓 Mon–Fri 9–5, Sat 9–1,
Sun 1–5. Treasury: Apr–Sep
daily 9–5; Oct–Mar 10–4.
Dome: Mar–Jun daily 10–5;
Jul, Aug 10–9; Sep–Oct 10–5
✋ Church: free. Tower/
Treasury: inexpensive
🍴 Café Kör (€€, ➤ 58)
Ⓜ M3 Arany János utca,
M1 Bajcsy-Zsilinszky út,
M1/2/3 Deák Ferenc tér

9 Szépművészeti Múzeum (Fine Arts Museum)

www.szepmuveszeti.hu

If any institution demonstrates Hungarians' appreciation of high art, it is this museum, which ranks as one of the major galleries in Central Europe.

With some 120,000 exhibits, the Fine Arts Museum holds the country's finest collection of foreign art. The building, designed by Albert Schickedanz and Fülöp Herzog and completed in 1906, represents the last piece of eclectic architecture in Hungary. The museum is ideally located in Heroes' Square (► 148–149), the grandest of Budapest's many open areas.

The Old Masters Gallery of the museum is world famous, exhibiting works by Raphael, Breughel, Rembrandt, El Greco, Goya and Velázquez, along with many more of the greats. British painting is well represented by Gainsborough, Hogarth and Reynolds. Also here are the French Impressionists and post-Impressionists, including works by Delacroix, Courbet, Millet, Gauguin, Renoir, Monet, Cézanne and Toulouse-Lautrec. Picasso, Chagall, Le Corbusier and Vasarely bring the French collection into the 20th century.

If you haven't had enough by this time, there's also the Ancient Egyptian art collection, which includes painted wooden mummy cases, fourth-century BC temple reliefs and some fine statuary. Be sure to take in the Greco-Roman collection and also the superb ceramics dating from the sixth to the first centuries BC.

✚ 9P ✉ Dózsa György út 41, Budapest XIV ☎ 469 7100
🕒 Tue–Sun 10–5:30 🍴 Moderate 🍴 Bagolyvàr (€€, ➤ 151)
Ⓜ M1 Hősök tere 🚌 Bus: 20E, 30, 105. Trolleybus: 75, 79
❓ Guided tours (in English): Tue–Fri 11 and 2, Sat 2. Charge for camera and video use

10 Vár-hegy (Castle Hill)

Set on a limestone outcrop overlooking the River Danube, this old residential quarter of Buda is a place of unrivalled charm.

Though the area dates from medieval times and earlier, little remains from this era – the result of successive wars and occupation by foreign powers. Painstaking reconstruction since World War II, when it was virtually destroyed, has, however, restored this part of Buda to a semblance of its once elegant baroque past. The wall of the castle is, in general, well preserved and offers a fine walk and spectacular views. Situated near the wall, close to Holy Trinity Column, is the statue of András Hadik (1710–90), "the most hussar of hussars", and the commander of Buda Castle. Close inspection of his horse's rear end reveals that its testicles are shiny yellow. Touched by generations of students – allegedly they bring good luck!

Houses 18, 20 and 22 on Országház utca (Országház Street), built in the 14th and 15th centuries, show what the Castle District might originally have looked like in medieval times, while on the corner of Országház utca and Kapisztrán tér (Kapisztrán Square) stands Mary Magdalene Tower (► 82–83), once a 13th-century church, and the only one allowed to remain a Christian church during Turkish rule. You will be hard-pressed to avoid the famous

Ruszwurm cafe (► 102) on Szentháromság utca
(Trinity Street), whose aromas have teased noses
since it opened in 1827.

Museums abound in the area, offering a variety
of interesting exhibitions: look for the Hadtörténeti
Múzeum (Museum of Military History, ► 82),
Telefónia Múzeum (Telephone Museum, ► 86),
Budavári Labirintus (Buda Castle Labyrinth, ► 77)
and Arany Sas Patikamúzeum (Golden Eagle
Pharmacy, ► 76). The Buda Royal Palace
(► 36–37) houses the Budapest History Museum
(► 78), the National Széchényi Library (► 80) and
the National Gallery (► 79).

✚ 1H ✉ Budapest I ⏱ Open access, except museums
✋ Free; admission charge for some museums (► 76–88)
🍴 Rivalda (€€€, ► 100) 🚌 Bus: 16, Várbusz. Funicular

Best things to do

Good places to have lunch 58–59

Top activities 60–61

Places to take the children 62–63

A walk around Nagykörút
(Grand Boulevard) 64–65

Best thermal baths 66–67

Stunning views 68–69

Best art nouveau 70–71

Good places to have lunch

Abszint (€€)

This simple yet stylish restaurant has an international menu blessed with a strong southern-French influence.

✉ Andrássy út 34, Budapest VI ☎ 332 4993; www.abszint.hu ⊙ Daily 11am–11:30pm

Café Kör (€€)

Enjoy modern Hungarian and European food served in generous portions and fine salad plates.

✉ Sas utca 17, Budapest V ☎ 311 0053; www.cafekor.com
⊙ Mon–Sat 10–10

Fatál (€€)

This traditional restaurant offers wholesome, home-style Hungarian dishes. The portions are generous and dishes are served on wooden plates. Payment by cash only.

✉ Váci utca 67 (entrance on Pintér utca), Budapest V ☎ 266 2607; www.fatalrestaurant.com ⊙ Daily 11:30am–2am

Gundel Étterem (€€€)

Hungary's most famous restaurant (► 147) is on the edge of City Park, by the Állatkert (zoo). Gundel has been restored to its *fin-de-siècle* splendour, and smart dress is required.

✉ Állatkerti körút 2, Budapest XIV ☎ 889 8100; www.gundel.hu ⊙ Daily 12–4, 6:30–12 (Sun brunch 11:30–3)

Kéhli (€€)

This authentic Hungarian restaurant caters for a mainly local clientele. It can be busy and you'll need to reserve if you prefer a table in the main dining area, which features a gypsy band.

✉ Mókus utca 22, Budapest III ☎ 250 4241/368 0613; www.kehli.hu
⊙ Daily 12–12

Kisbuda Gyöngye (€€)

The restaurant is typically Hungarian, magnificently styled in early 20th-century bourgeois affectation, with a genial piano-violin duo setting the mood. There's a rich and varied menu.

✉ Kenyeres utca 34, Budapest III ☎ 368 6402; www.remiz.hu
🕔 Tue–Sat 12–11

Malomtó (€€–€€€)

Malomtó scores high for its location and food. Choose from a range of imaginative international options, while relaxing next to the adjacent small lake. Once you've finished, scoot around the lake and take a peek at the Turkish bathhouse ruins.

✉ Frankel Leó út 48, Budapest II
☎ 336 1830 🕔 Daily 12–12

Múzeum (€€)

Múzeum is still going strong after more than a hundred years and serves solid Hungarian fare in beautifully preserved *fin-de-siècle* surroundings. Look for the ceiling fresco by Károly Lotz.

✉ Múzeum körút 12, Budapest VIII ☎ 267 0375; www.muzeumkavehaz.hu
🕔 Mon–Sat 12–11

Robinson (€€–€€€)

The Robinson is romantically located on the lake by Heroes' Square, and its decked terrace stretches out onto the lake itself. The menu contains Hungarian and international dishes.

✉ Városliget Lake, Budapest XIV ☎ 422 0222; www.robinsonrestaurant.hu
🕔 Daily 12–5, 6–12

Top activities

Board a narrow-gauge train: The Cogwheel Railway (➤ 173) and the Children's Railway (➤ 62) offer an atmospheric way to explore the Buda Hills.

Step back in time: Wander the ancient Roman ruins at Aquincum (➤ 94).

Get up close to communism: Visit Memento Park, where you can see many of the imposing communist statues that once dominated the city's streets (➤ 175).

Enjoy a festival: There are superb festivals throughout the year, with the summer and autumn festivals particular highlights (▶ 24–25).

Look around a museum: Budapest has some wonderful museums and galleries, including the Hungarian National Museum (▶ 160–161) and the Hungarian National Gallery (▶ 79).

Take a boat trip on the Danube: One of the best ways to see the city is from the water (www.mahartpassnave.hu).

Seek out specialist stores: There's great shopping in Belváros and along Váci útca (▶ 130–135).

Ride tram 2: The route along the Danube banks is a quick and easy way to catch a glimpse of many of Budapest's biggest attractions (▶ 28).

Walk around Vár-hegy: Set a day aside to explore the Castle District on foot (▶ 54–55).

Go for a stroll: Around car-free Margitsziget and the scenic Budai-hegyek (▶ 44–45,173–174).

Take to the waters: A dip in one of the city's thermal baths is a treat not to be missed (▶ 66–67).

Spend a night at the opera: Take in one of the performances at the Magyar Állami Operaház (▶ 42–43).

Visit Városliget: The City Park is a prime picnicking spot and has an outdoor ice rink in winter (▶ 146).

Places to take the children

Állatkert (Municipal Zoo)

One of the oldest zoos in the world also has 3,500 plant species.

✉ Állatkerti körút 6–12, Budapest XIV ☎ 273 4901; www.zoobudapest.com
🕐 May–Aug Mon–Thu 9–6:30, Fri–Sun 9–7; Apr, Sep Mon–Thu 9–5:30, Fri–Sun
9–6; Mar, Oct Mon–Thu 9–5, Fri–Sun 9–5.30; Nov–Feb daily 9–4 👍 Expensive
🚇 M1 Széchenyi fürdő 🚌 Bus: 20E, 30, 30A, 105. Trolleybus: 72, 79

Budapest Bábszínház (Budapest Puppet Theatre)

The shows are in Hungarian but children love them all the same.

✉ Andrássy út 69, Budapest VI ☎ 321 5200; www.budapestbabszinhaz.hu
🕐 Shows usually Mon–Fri 10, Sat–Sun 3 👍 Moderate–expensive
🚇 M1 Vörösmarty utca

Csodák Palotája: Interaktív Tudományos Játszóház
(Palace of Miracles: Interactive Scientific Playhouse)

More than 100 spectacular, hands-on games and experiments.

✉ Fény utca 20–22, Budapest II ☎ 350 6131; www.millenaris.hu/csodak-
palotaja 🕐 Mon–Fri 9–5, Sat–Sun 10–6. Closed 1 Jan, Easter Mon, 1 Nov,
24–26, 31 Dec 👍 Expensive 🚇 M2 Moszkva tér

Fővárosi Nagycirkusz (Municipal Circus)

World-famous Hungarian trapeze artists, plus clowns and animals.

✉ Állatkerti körút 12, Budapest XIV ☎ 343 8300; www.maciva.hu 🕐 Shows
Mar to mid-Jun Wed–Fri 3, Sat 11, 7, Sun 11, 3; Jul–Aug Wed–Thu 5, Fri–Sat
3, 7, Sun 11, 3 👍 Expensive 🚇 M1 Széchenyi fürdő 🚌 Trolleybus 72

Gyermekvasút (Children's Railway)

Narrow-gauge railway running along an 11km (8-mile) route and
supervised (in addition to the driver) by uniformed local children.
The train calls at János Hill, the city's highest point.

✉ Hegyhát út, Budapest X ☎ 397 5392; www.gyermekvasut.hu 🕐 Mid-Mar
to Oct Mon–Fri 10–5, Sat–Sun 9:45–5:30; Nov to mid-Mar Tue–Fri 10–4,
Sat–Sun 10–5 👍 One-way: inexpensive; round-trip: moderate 🚌 Bus: 22, 90,
90A, 222. Tram: 61, Hűvösvölgy

Libegő (Chairlift)

The 15-minute trip between Zugliget and János Hill offers unforgettable views.

⊠ Zugligeti út 93, Budapest ⊕ Apr to mid-Sep daily 9:30–5; mid-Sep to Apr daily 9:30–4:30 🖐 One-way: moderate; round-trip: expensive 🚌 Bus: 291

Planetárium

The largest Hungarian institution of public education on space exploration and astronomy.

⊠ Népliget, Budapest X ☎ 263 1811; www.planetarium.hu

⊕ Tue–Sun 9:30–5; English-language show Tue at 4

🖐 Expensive 🚇 M3 Népliget

Sikló (Funicular)

Running between Clark Ádám tér and Buda Royal Palace. The ride lasts only two minutes, but it's fun.

⊠ Clark Ádám tér, Budapest

☎ 201 9128 ⊕ Daily 7:30am–10pm. Closed 1st and 3rd Mon

🖐 Moderate–expensive

🚌 Bus: 16. Tram: 19, 41

Vidámpark (Amusement Park)

Funfair attractions, plus a restored 19th-century carousel.

⊠ Állatkerti körút 14–16, Budapest XIV ☎ 363 8310; www.vidampark.hu

⊕ May–Aug daily 10–8; Mar–Apr, Sep Sat–Sun 12–6 🚇 M1 Széchenyi fürdő 🖐 Expensive 🚌 Trolleybus: 72

a walk around Nagykörút (Grand Boulevard)

This is the longest thoroughfare of the city, running from Petőfi híd in the south to Margit híd in the north. It changes names five times along the way, representing the five districts it traverses; Ferenc körút in district IX, József körút in VIII, Erzsébet körút in VII, Teréz körút in VI and Szent István körút in XIII.

Start at Boráros tér by Petőfi Bridge heading towards Ferenc körút.

On your left are three large blocks of pre-World War II apartments and between them on Bakáts tér the beautiful spired Ferencváros Parish Church.

Continue up Ferenc körút to Üllői út and the Museum of Applied Arts (▶ 162). Cross Üllői út, and on your right is the Corvin Cinema, the head-quarters of armed resistance during the 1956 Uprising. Now you're on József körút. On your way to Rákóczi tér, on the right, look out for the War Memorial.

Rákóczi tér, once a playground for Budapest's seedier side, has been cleaned up somewhat but still retains a semblance of colour.

Farther on up the tree-lined boulevard, on the right, is Blaha Lujza tér, one of the city's central squares. Cross Rákóczi út, and head for the New York Kávéház (New York Café), restored to its original glory. Now you're on Erzsébet körút. The Grand Hotel Royal is on your right. A short walk farther on is Teréz körút; just off this is the Academy of Music (➤ 141).

On the right where Andrássy út joins the Oktogon is the copy of Florentine Palazzo Strozz.

A little farther on, with the Radisson Blu Béke Hotel on the right, you arrive at Nyugati tér, with the finely restored Western Railway Station (➤ 139–140). Cross Üllői út. On your right, at Szent István körút, is the Vígszínház theatre. A short walk along on the right takes you to Margaret Bridge and the Danube, where this walk ends.

Distance 4.5km (3 miles)
Time 4–5 hours, 6 hours with stops
Start point Boráros tér ✚ 8X 🚋 Tram: 2
End point Margit híd (Margaret Bridge) ✚ 3E 🚋 Tram: 2
Lunch New York Kávéház (New York Café, ➤ 155)

Best thermal baths

Csillaghegy

The city's oldest open-air bath, with three pools and parkland.
✉ Pusztakúti út 3, Budapest III ☎ 250 1533 🖐 Expensive 🚌 Bus: 42
🚊 HÉV Csillaghegy

Dagály

A massive complex with 10 pools, some of which are filled with warm thermal water.

✉ Népfürdő utca 36, Budapest XIII ☎ 452 4556 👋 Expensive Ⓜ M3 Árpád híd 🚌 Bus: 133. Tram: 1

Gellért
This art nouveau gem has both indoor and outdoor pools (➤ 107).

Health Spa Resort
This modern spa, in the Danubius Health Spa Resort Margitsziget, is in a lovely setting on Budapest's favourite island.
✉ Margitsziget, Budapest XIII ☎ 889 4737 👋 Expensive 🚌 Bus: 26

Király
Király has a wonderful sky-lit cupola (➤ 92).

Lukács
The neoclassical complex has indoor and outdoor thermal pools.
✉ Frankel Leó utca 25–29, Budapest II ☎ 326 1695 👋 Expensive
🚌 Bus: 86

Rác
An original Turkish bath with a 19th-century facade, Rác is undergoing renovation to create a luxury hotel spa complex.
✉ Hadnagy utca 8–10, Budapest I 🚋 Tram: 18, 19

Rudas
A classic Turkish bath dating from 1566, Rudas (➤ 110) has a domed octagonal room, atmospheric surrounds and a neoclassical wing.
✉ Döbrentei tér 9, Budapest I ☎ 356 1322 👋 Expensive 🚌 Bus: 5, 7, 8, 86. Tram: 18, 19 ❓ Women allowed only on Tue, Sat–Sun; late opening Fri–Sat

Széchenyi
Neoclassical in design, Széchenyi is a gorgeous outdoor arena with its fair share of indoor pools and thermal treatments (➤ 147).

Stunning views

From Vár-hegy (Castle Hill, ➤ 54), particularly from Halászbástya (Fishermen's Bastion, ➤ 40–41).

From Gellért-hegy (Gellért Hill, ➤ 38–39) over Pest and Vár-hegy.

From the Citadella (➤ 106).

From Erzsébet-kilátó (Elizabeth tower) on János-hegy (➤ 174).

From the dome of Szent István Bazilika (St Stephen's Basilica, ➤ 50–51).

From the terrace of Peppers! Restaurant, Mariott Hotel (Apáczai Csere János utca 4, Budapest V).

From the Watertower on Margitsziget (Margaret Island ➤ 44–45).

From the Sikló (Funicular, ➤ 84) leading up to Buda Royal Palace.

From Dunakorzó (➤ 117) across to Buda and its Danube embankment.

From tram 2 along the Pest embankment (➤ 28).

Best art nouveau

Állatkert (Zoo) The entranceway and elephant house of the Állatkert are unmistakable examples of art nouveau (➤ 62).

Bedő Ház (Bedő House) Not an extravagant structure, but its unusual facade, with flower designs, grumpy faces and individual window frames, is highly appealing. ✉ Honvéd utca 3, Budapest V

Földtani Intézet (Geology Institute) Look for its mesmerizing blue-tiled roof and stunning interior. ✉ Stefánia út 14, Budapest XIV

Gresham Palace A beautifully restored example of secessionist (Hungarian art nouveau) architecture (➤ 122–123).

Gellért Gyógyfürdő (Gellért Thermal Baths) One of the few examples of art nouveau on the Buda side of the river (➤ 107–108).

Iparművészeti Múzeum (Museum of Applied Arts) Features an exterior of Zsolnay ceramic tiles and Moorish design (➤ 162).

Magyar Királyi Takarékpénztár (Former Royal Post Office Savings Bank) Hungarian folk art motifs, art nouveau swirls, a lime-green roof, and even a swarm of bees (➤ 123).

Thonet Ház (Thonet House) Another designed by Ödön Lechner – who is also responsible for the Museum of Applied Arts, the Royal Savings Bank and the Geology Institute – with generous use of Zsolnay tiles and floral motifs. ✉ Váci utca 11, Budapest V

Török Bankház (Turkish Bank House) Unexceptional until you encounter its gable, filled with a mosaic by Miksa Róth depicting Hungary paying homage to the Virgin Mary. ✉ Szervita tér 3, Budapest V

Zeneakadémia (Academy of Music) As interiors go, the Zeneakadémia is hard to beat (➤ 141).

Exploring

Vár-hegy, Víziváros and Óbuda   75–104

Gellért-hegy and the Tabán   105–114

Belváros and Lipótváros   115–136

Terézváros, Erzsébetváros and
Városliget   137–158

Józsefváros and Ferencváros   159–169

Not until 1873, when the three districts of Buda, Pest and Óbuda (Old Buda) were amalgamated, did the capital city of Budapest come into existence. The first major settlement here was Aquincum, built by the Romans. Remains of their aqueduct and amphitheatres are just north of Óbuda. Buda, an important centre of Renaissance learning during the 16th century, fell into decline during the 150 years of Turkish occupation. One legacy of the Turks was their thermal baths, which are an unmissable treat. On the eastern bank of the Danube, Pest only came into prominence in the 19th century. Once Hungary had wrested virtual autonomy from the Habsburgs in the Compromise of 1867, this part of the city expanded rapidly to the east of the Danube. By 1896, united Budapest had become a great metropolitan centre, with a thriving cultural life that still reverberates today in a host of venues of all kinds.

Vár-hegy, Víziváros and Óbuda

Nothing in Budapest is as dominant as Vár-hegy (Castle Hill). This lofty limestone plateau rising above the Danube is an arresting sight, topped by a walled medieval town containing some of the city's greatest sights. Between Vár-hegy and the fast-flowing Danube is Víziváros (Watertown) and to the north lies Óbuda (Old Buda), Budapest's ancient heart.

Vár-hegy is home to the former Hungarian royal quarters (Budai Királyi Palota, ➤ 36), the unique Mátyás-templom (Matthias Church, ➤ 46), and a good collection of informative and unusual museums.

Simply wandering its quiet, cobblestone streets (only residents can drive here) is as pleasurable as seeing any big attraction.

Nearby Víziváros is a long, thin district with a subdued atmosphere and an intriguing past. Its foundations were laid by the Romans and reminders of the Turkish occupation are dotted throughout the area.

Óbuda also has a long history; while now a quiet corner of the city, it was here that the Romans established the town of Aquincum almost 2,000 years ago.

Vár-hegy

ARANY SAS PATIKAMÚZEUM (GOLDEN EAGLE PHARMACY)

Its current neoclassical facade may date from 1820, but the Arany Sas Patikamúzeum occupies a 15th-century building in the heart of the Castle District. It is the first pharmacy established in Buda after the expulsion of the Turks and contains an unusual collection of archaic pharmaceutical paraphernalia, including a mock laboratory. Note the painting of the nun – during the Middle Ages it was their job to perform the task of a chemist.

www.semmelweis.museum.hu/aranysas

✚ 2H ✉ Tárnok utca 18, Budapest I ☎ 375 9772 ⊕ Apr–Sep Tue–Sun 10:30–5:30; Oct–Mar Tue–Sun 10:30–3:30 ✋ Inexpensive 🍴 Ruszwurm (€, ➤ 102) 🚌 Bus: 16, Várbusz

BÉCSI KAPU (VIENNA GATE)

The Vienna Gate is where all four streets that run the length of Castle Hill converge, and in the Middle Ages this was the place of the "Saturday Market" for non-Jewish merchant traders. The story goes that any loud-mouthed Hungarian child would be scolded by being told his mouth was "as big as the Vienna Gate".

Climb to the top of the gate and enjoy the panorama of Buda and the view of the Lutheran church in the square. There are also fine views of the Parliament building across the Danube. Next to the bastion wall, to the right of the gate, is a small grove, the "Europe Grove". It gets its name from the time when the mayors of cities all over Europe brought and planted rare trees here – for example, Turkish hazel, Japanese cherry and cherry laurel.

✚ 1G ✉ Castle District, Budapest I ⏱ Open access 🍴 Café Pierrot (€€, ➤ 98) 🚌 Bus: Várbusz ❓ Cars are not allowed to enter the Castle District without a permit

BUDAVÁRI LABIRINTUS (CASTLE LABYRINTH)

The entrance on Úri utca 9 leads to an underground labyrinth stretching for about 10km (6 miles) beneath Castle Hill. These fascinating caves were joined together by the Turks for military purposes and today a section of about 1.5km (1 mile) can be explored. A waxwork exhibition (not to everyone's taste) is located here – a memorial of Hungarian history that is both light-hearted and serious. The exhibition recounts Hungary's mythological beginnings and finishes in the flourishing Renaissance Court of King Matthias. Oddly, nothing of Hungary's more recent, perhaps less glorious, times is included. Only a street sign on the wall recalls the bitter years of World War II when thousands of people took refuge here from the siege. The Castle Labyrinth is not recommended for those who suffer from claustrophobia.

www.labirintus.com

✚ 2H ✉ Úri utca 9, Budapest I ☎ 489 3281 ⏱ Daily 9:30–7:30 💰 Expensive 🍴 Miró (€, ➤ 102) 🚌 Bus: 16, Várbusz. Funicular ❓ Guided tours only

BUDAI KIRÁLYI PALOTA (BUDA ROYAL PALACE)

Best places to see, ➤ 36–37.

Budapesti Történeti Múzeum (Budapest History Museum)

Occupying the southern end of the Buda Royal Palace, this excellent exhibition provides a historical record of Budapest's last 2,000 years. In the basement front hall of the history museum there's a plaster model of Castle Hill, as well as a detailed black-and-white drawing of the Gothic Buda Royal Palace as it probably used to be. Its largest hall was 70m (76yds) by 17m (19yds), big enough even for horseback tournaments to take place within it! The museum is divided into two sections. On the lower level (a maze of passageways, cellars and vaulted halls) can be seen the remains of the medieval palace, together with sculptures, pots, pans and weapons. Above is the principal exhibition, documenting Budapest's long history, and containing photographs, prints and posters and, perhaps surprisingly, artefacts from the Turkish occupation.

www.btm.hu

🔢 3J ✉ Budai Királyi Palota (Wing E), Budapest I ☎ 487 8800 🕐 Mar–Oct Tue–Sun 10–6; Nov–Feb Tue–Sun 10–4 ✋ Moderate 🍴 Rivalda (€€€, ➤ 100) 🚌 Bus: 16, Várbusz. Funicular

Luthertől

Magyar Nemzeti Galéria (Hungarian National Gallery)

This huge and richly stocked gallery traces the evolution of the arts in Hungary from the Middle Ages to the 20th century. It's too much to take in at one time; concentrate on a few treasures, such as the medieval altarpieces. Hungarian history is amply illustrated in large canvases of heroic deeds. Perhaps the most appealing sections deal with the late 19th and early 20th centuries, when Hungarian artists made a significant contribution to the Impressionist and art nouveau movements. Look for works by the sensitive József Rippl-Rónai, while the wayward Tivadar Kosztka Csontváry is in his own category, with a highly personal symbolism.

www.mng.hu/en

✚ 3J ✉ Budai Királyi Palota (Wings B, C and D), Budapest I ☎ 06 20 4397 325
🕐 Tue–Sun 10–6 👋 Moderate
🚌 Bus: 16, Várbusz. Funicular ❓ Tours

Mátyás-Kút (Matthias Well)

Placed against a north-facing wall of the Buda Royal Palace, the well has a bronze statue of King Matthias as a huntsman in the

company of his shield bearer and Italian chronicler. The statue
includes the figure of Szép Ilona (Helen the Fair), a beautiful
peasant girl who fell in love with the king while he was hunting
– a case of unrequited love.

➕ 3J ✉ Szent György tér, Budapest I 🎟 Open access 🚌 Bus: 16, Várbusz.
Funicular

Országos Széchényi Könyvtár (National Széchényi Library)

Yet another major site in the Buda Royal Palace, this library stocks
over 2 million books, and even more manuscripts, musical scores
and newspapers. Among these are the few remaining codices
(manuscript volumes) from King Matthias's celebrated library. The
codices are called Corvinas, and refer to the raven – the King's
heraldic emblem. The Main Reading Room, made up of several
smaller rooms, is spacious but not especially elegant.

www.oszk.hu

➕ 3J ✉ Budai Királyi Palota (Wing F), Budapest I ☎ 224 3845
🎟 Sep–Jul Tue–Sat 10–9. Closed Aug 💵 Moderate 🚌 Bus: 16, Várbusz.
Funicular

Savoyai Jenő szobor (Statue of Eugene of Savoy)

Opposite the entrance to Buda Royal Palace on the Danube side
is the powerful equestrian statue of Prince Eugene of Savoy
(1663–1736). Born in Paris, following his father's death and his
mother's subsequent banishment from the French court by Louis
XIV, the prince renounced the country of his birth and joined the
service of Emperor Leopold I in the fight against the Turks. In a
distinguished career he inflicted a series of defeats on the Turks;
in 1697 at Zenta on the River Tisza, in 1716 at Petrovaradin and
Temesvár (now Timisoara), and in 1717 at Belgrade, where his
force of 40,000 overcame an army of nearly 250,000 and Eugene
was wounded for the 13th time.

➕ 3J ✉ Front entrance, Budai Királyi Palota, Budapest I 🚌 Bus: 16,
Várbusz. Funicular

HADTÖRTÉNETI MÚZEUM
(MUSEUM OF MILITARY HISTORY)

Facing the Buda Hills, this museum is devoted to Hungary's military history. While it looks like the kind of museum where static displays might sit and collect dust, it actually does a fine job of covering the country's military exploits against occupying forces and during the two world wars by showing uniforms, weapons and other memorabilia. Special sections on the 1848–49 revolution and the 1956 Uprising are enlightening, and the oft-forgotten period just after World War I – when the "Red Army" travelled through the country acting as a death squad – is quite shocking. A handful of displays are complemented by English explanations, and there are tours in English and German.

www.militaria.hu

🔡 1G 🖂 Tóth Árpád sétány 40, Budapest I ☎ 325 1600 🕓 Apr–Sep Tue–Sun 10–6; Oct–Mar 10–4
💲 Inexpensive 🍴 Café Pierrot (€€, ➤ 98) 🚌 Bus: 16, Várbusz

HALÁSZBÁSTYA
(FISHERMEN'S BASTION)

Best places to see, ➤ 40–41.

MÁRIA MAGDOLNA-TORONY (MARY MAGDALENE TOWER)

This 13th-century church was built for Hungarian worshippers on the border of a German parish. Today only the tower, some foundations and a reconstructed arched window remain. During Turkish rule special dispensation was given to the church to allow it to remain

Christian, while all other churches were converted to mosques. Unfortunately the chancel and nave were destroyed during World War II, and have not been rebuilt, except for one stone window as a memento. Worthy of note are the serried ranks of 24 bells. Their chime, a modern addition, sounds like tumbling icicles.

✚ 1G ✉ Kapisztrán tér, Budapest I (on the corner of Országház utca)
✋ Free 🚌 Bus: 16, Várbusz

MÁTYÁS-TEMPLOM (MATTHIAS CHURCH)

Best places to see, ➤ 46–47.

ORSZÁGHÁZ UTCA 18, 20, 22

Built in the 14th and 15th centuries, these three houses show what the Castle District may have looked like in the Middle Ages. Italian craftsmen working on the Royal Palace once lived here. The initials inscribed on the gate of the middle house are those of Johann Nicki, the butcher who had the house rebuilt in 1771.

✚ 1G ✉ Országház utca 18, 20, 22, Budapest I 🍴 Miró (€, ➤ 102)
🚌 Bus: 16, Várbusz

RÉGI BUDAI VÁROSHÁZA (OLD TOWN HALL)

This imposingly quaint building, formerly the seat of the city's council, is now the Institute for Advanced Study. The first session of the Council was held here in 1710, but its governing function came to an end in 1873 when Buda and Pest were united. The fine proportions of the Old Town Hall's windows and inner forked staircase suggest erstwhile political harmony. The statue (actually an Italian copy) on the corner of the building represents Pallas Athene, the guardian of towns. Reminiscent of some of the smaller Oxford colleges, this is a bustling place during term time. Don't feel reticent about visiting it during this time, as the students and staff are most welcoming.

🚩 2H ✉ Szentháromság utca 2, Budapest I 🕐 Officially not open to the public, but visitors welcome 🚌 Bus: 16, Várbusz. Funicular

SIKLÓ (FUNICULAR)

This is not just worth seeing, but is also fun to ride. Opened to the public in 1870, like the rest of the Castle District it suffered severe damage during World War II, and was rebuilt in 1986. Originally the railway was steam powered and adroitly used the weight of the passengers and car going downwards to pull the other car upwards. You can enjoy a wonderful view of the Pest area from the funicular. The ride from the Buda end of the Chain Bridge up to Castle Hill takes two minutes. The car also carries prams (strollers) and wheelchairs.

🚩 3J ✉ Clark Ádám tér (lower terminus), Szent György tér (upper terminus), Budapest I 🕐 Daily 7:30am–10pm. Closed every other Mon 🖐 One-way moderate; round-trip expensive 🚌 Bus: 16. Tram 19, 41

SZÉCHENYI LÁNCHÍD (SZÉCHENYI CHAIN BRIDGE)

A symbol of Budapest and the first bridge over the Danube, this bridge was built between 1839 and 1849 on the initiative of Count István Széchenyi. It was designed by Englishman William Tierney Clark, and built by his namesake, the Scotsman Adam Clark.

During the country's War of Independence, the first carriage to cross the bridge (at a time when it was still under construction) carried the Hungarian crown from Buda, which was then under siege, to Debrecen. Later, the Austrian troops decided to blow the bridge up – but the ever-resourceful Adam Clark frustrated their attempt by flooding the explosive-packed chain chambers with water. However, the Széchenyi Chain Bridge was eventually blown up during World War II. It reopened again on 20 November 1949, exactly 100 years after its original inauguration.

✚ 3H ✉ Clark Ádám tér, Budapest I to Roosevelt tér, Budapest V 🍴 Seoul House (€, ➤ 100) 🚌 Bus: 16. Tram: 2, 19, 41

SZENTHÁROMSÁG SZOBOR
(HOLY TRINITY COLUMN)

In the middle of Szentháromság tér near Matthias Church, the highest point on Castle Hill, the 14m-tall (46ft) monument was erected between 1710 and 1713 by the inhabitants of Buda. It was hoped that the column would fend off further plague epidemics.

🚇 2H 🖂 Szentháromság tér, Budapest I 🍴 Ruszwurm (€, ➤ 102) 🚌 Bus: 16, Várbusz

TELEFÓNIA MÚZEUM
(TELEPHONE MUSEUM)

The enlightening little Telephone Museum tells the history of the phone in Budapest, and is a startling reminder of the speed at which technology has developed. In 1882, Budapest was the third city in Europe to install a telephone exchange (after London and Paris). The museum premises were used as a secondary exchange from 1928 to 1985. The huge exchange is still in working order; if it's not too busy the ticket attendant will flip a switch to make it whiz and burr. A second room houses some public phones (the first was installed in Belváros in 1928) and the first mobiles; produced by Motorola and Ericsson, the latter look more like small suitcases than the handy little devices we use today. Bizarrely, there's also a small shrine to Gábor Dénes (1900–79), inventor of the hologram and 1971 Nobel Prize winner. The museum overlooks a peaceful inner courtyard – a fine spot to escape the castle's summer crowds.

www.postamuzeum.hu

🚇 1G 🖂 Úri utca 49, Budapest I (at weekends entrance is via Országház utca 30) ☎ 201 8188 🕐 Tue–Sun 10–4 💷 Inexpensive 🚌 Bus: 16

ÚRI UTCA
(LORDS' STREET)

This street runs the length of the Castle District. The facades of its houses are later additions, but the courtyards, ground floors, gateways with their recessed benches, and cellars are medieval. This is a place where you can literally step into the past.

➕ 2H ✉ Úri utca, Budapest I 🍴 Miró (€, ➤ 102) 🚌 Bus: 16, Várbusz. Funicular

VÁR-HEGY (CASTLE HILL)

Best places to see, ➤ 54–55.

VÁRSZÍNHÁZ (CASTLE THEATRE)

Completed in 1736, the building was originally the Church of the Order of Our Lady of Mount Carmel, but in 1784 Joseph II dissolved this order. The monastery became a casino and the church gave way to a theatre. The theatre had a wooden floor and could seat 1,200. It was here that the first play in Hungarian was performed – previous performances had been in German. In 1942 part of the gallery collapsed – the next performance wasn't until 1978, when the new theatre, of marble and concrete (seating 252 people), opened. It houses the Nemzeti Táncszínház (National Dance Theatre, ➤ 104).

www.nemzetitancszinhaz.hu

➕ 2H ✉ Színház utca 1–3, Budapest I 🕐 Daily
☎ 201 4407 or 375 8649 🍴 Rivalda (€€€, ➤ 100)
🚌 Bus: 16, Várbusz. Funicular

a walk around Vár-hegy (Castle Hill)

This walk round Castle Hill (➤ 54) gives a taste of the old town of Buda.

From Dísz tér (Dísz Square) enter Tárnok utca.

At No 18 is the Patikamúzeum (Museum of Pharmacy, ➤ 76), a former chemist's shop dating from 1745.

Walk towards Szentháromság tér. Pass to the right of Matthias Church (➤ 46–47) into cobbled courtyards with the Halászbástya (Fishermen's Bastion, ➤ 40–41) in front of you.

Climb the towers of the Fishermen's Bastion for spectacular views of the Danube and Pest.

Return via the north side of Matthias Church with the Hilton Hotel on your right. Back on Szentháromság tér, turn right into Hess András tér, then bear left and walk down Fortuna utca.

Fortuna utca is perhaps the most picturesque street on Castle Hill.

Passing the Café Pierrot (▶ 98), enter Bécsikapu tér, dominated by the neo-Romanesque edifice of the National Archives of Hungary. Walk up Petermann Bíró utca to the tower and ruins of medieval Mary Magdalene Church (▶ 82–83), dating from the 13th century, then turn left towards Úri utca.

The pastel-green building on the right, with a police sign outside, houses the Telefónia Múzeum (Telephone Museum, ▶ 86).

Return to Szentháromság tér. Turn left by the equestrian statue of Hadik András to Tóth Árpád sétány for distant views of the Buda Hills. Turn back, then right onto Úri utca.

At No 9 is the entrance to the Castle Labyrinth (▶ 77). Many of the caves are believed to be between 500 and 700 years old and were used for military purposes by occupying Turks.

Stroll down into Dísz tér, where the walk ends.

Distance Approx 1km (0.6 miles)
Time 1 hour, or 2 hours with stops
Start/end point Disz tér ✚ 2H
▣ Várbusz. Funicular from Szent György tér
Lunch Rivalda (€€€, ▶ 100)

Víziváros

KIRÁLY GYÓGYFÜRDŐ (KING THERMAL BATHS)

One of the most famous thermal baths in Hungary, this is where to come for a course of complete revitalization. Besides the thermal pool, there are tub baths, salt baths and massage and sauna services. Built on a former Roman military road, the baths were constructed by the Turkish Pasha of Buda, Arslan, in the 16th century. They were then bought by the König family. *König* means "King" in German, from which the name *Király* ("King" in Hungarian) stems. The building's Turkish decor and styling, especially the cupolas, make it an architectural masterpiece.

www.budapestgyogyfurdoi.hu

✚ 2F ✉ Fő utca 84, Budapest II
☎ 202 3688 🍴 Cafe (€) 🕐 Men: Tue, Thu, Sat 10–10. Women: Mon, Fri 8–8. Mixed: Wed, Sun 8–8 ✋ Expensive Ⓜ M2 Batthyány tér 🚌 Bus: 60, 86

ÖNTÖDEI MÚZEUM (FOUNDRY MUSEUM)

Built on the site of the old Ganz ironworks, which produced the world's first electric railway engine, the museum has a reconstructed foundry and workshop, and a collection of products once manufactured here.
www.omm.hu

🔢 2F ✉ Bem József utca 20, Budapest II ☎ 201 4370
🕐 Tue–Sun 9–5 🍴 Kacsa (€€, ➤ 98) 🎫 Inexpensive 🚇 M2
Batthyány tér 🚌 Bus: 11, 60, 86. Tram: 4, 6

SZENT ANNA TEMPLOM

St Anne's Church is the finest example of baroque architecture in the city. Commissioned by the Jesuits in 1740, it took another 65 years to be consecrated due to some major delays – it suffered earthquake damage in 1763 and the dissolution of the Jesuit order in 1773, and World War II saw the facade sustain more damage. The highlight of the rich baroque facade is the Buda coat of arms, which is topped by two kneeling angels and the Trinity symbol. Inside, statues of St Anne presenting Mary to the Temple of Jerusalem complement the concave High Altar, which rises to the central frescoed dome. Also of note are the 1768 dark side altar and the cherub-topped organ.

www.szentannaplebania.hu

🔢 3F ✉ Batthyány tér 7, Budapest II
☎ 201 6364 🕐 Services: Mon–Fri
6:30am, 5pm, Sat 7:30am, 6pm, Sun
7:30am, 9am, 10am, 11am, 6pm
🎫 Free 🍴 Angelika (€, ➤ 101)
🚇 M2 Batthyány tér

Óbuda

AQUINCUM

Once a bustling Roman town established in the first century AD, Aquincum is today a collection of grassy areas and sectioned ruins. Most of the finds, uncovered in the late 19th century, are in the site's museum. Pottery, weapons, jewellery, coins and mosaics are the mainstay of the collection, but don't miss the water-powered organ that has been restored to working order. Of the scattered ruins, the public baths and Macellum, the town's covered market, are the most intact.

www.aquincum.hu

🚶 3A (off map) ✉ Szentendrei út 135, Budapest III ☎ 250 1650 🕐 May–Sep Tue–Sun 9–6; 15–30 Apr, Oct 9–5; Nov–14 Apr 10–4 ✋ Moderate 🍴 Cafe (€) 🚌 Bus: 34, 106, 134 🚆 HÉV Aquincum

ÁRPÁD HÍD (ÁRPÁD BRIDGE)

North of Margaret Bridge, Árpád Bridge is the longest and most robust of the six

bridges crossing the Danube in the vicinity of downtown Budapest and links the mainland with Margaret Island (➤ 44–45). It's worth a walk across if only for the views it offers of the city and a sense of the immense breadth of the Danube, and Margaret Island certainly merits a visit.

➕ 6A ✉ Árpád híd, Budapest III
🍴 Kéhli (€€, ➤ 58) 🚌 Bus: 26. Tram: 1

HERCULES VILLA

The Hercules Villa refers not to a building but to a series of third-century AD mosaic floors discovered hidden among a block of residential flats in the late 1950s. In extremely good condition considering their age, the mosaics depict Hercules firing an arrow into centaur Nessos as he takes flight with Deianeira. The detailed work (some 60,000 stones) was probably brought to Buda from Alexandria already arranged and ready to go.

➕ 3A (off map) ✉ Meggyfa utca 19–21, Budapest III ☎ 250 1650 🕐 15 Apr–30 Oct by appointment only. Closed rest of year
💰 Expensive 🍴 Új Sipos Halászkert (€€, ➤ 101) 🚌 Bus: 86

MARGITSZIGET (MARGARET ISLAND)

Best places to see, ➤ 44–45.

HOTELS

art'otel (€€€)

In the picturesque Víziváros area between the Danube and Castle Hill, the "art hotel" is a wonderful synthesis of immaculately restored 18th-century fishermen's dwellings and 21st-century designer rooms featuring the work of New Yorker Donald Sultan.

✉ Bem rakpart 16–19, Budapest I ☎ 487 9487; www.artotel.hu

Buda Castle Hotel (€€€)

This four-star superior fashion hotel is in the Castle District, a stone's throw from Matthias Church. The rooms are on the large side and rates aren't bad considering the prime location.

✉ Úri utca 39, Budapest I ☎ 224 7900; www.budacastlehotelbudapest.com

Burg Hotel (€€)

The Burg is bang in the middle of the Castle District, offering a cheaper option in the area. The rooms are no-frills but comfortable. Another plus is free parking for guests inside the castle gates.

✉ Szentháromság tér 7–8, Budapest I ☎ 212 0269; www.burghotelbudapest.com

Danubius Grand Hotel Margitsziget (€€€)

This old, four-star spa hotel shares a beautiful setting with the Danubius Health Spa Resort (► below) on leafy Margaret Island in the middle of the Danube and relatively close to the city centre.

✉ Margitsziget, Budapest XIII ☎ 889 4700; www.danubiushotels.com

Danubius Health Spa Resort Margitsziget (€€€)

This spa hotel is much less elegant than the Danubius Grand (► above), but the location on Margaret Island is very attractive, as is its four-star rating. The spa receives natural spring water from the island.

✉ Margitsziget, Budapest XIII ☎ 889 4700; www.danubiushotels.com

Hilton Hotel (€€€)

A pearl in the Hilton chain, this modern hotel in the Castle District blends tastefully with its picturesque surroundings and, naturally,

offers high standards all round. The ICON Restaurant (➤ 98) is
first class.

✉ Hess András tér 1–3, Budapest I ☎ 889 6600; www.budapest.hilton.com

Hotel Budapest (€€€)

A large, cylinder-shaped hotel within walking distance of Castle
Hill, this is a conference-oriented hotel that offers fine panoramic
views of Buda.

✉ Szilágyi Erzsébet fasor 47, Budapest I ☎ 889 4200;
www.danubiushotels.com

Lánchíd 19 (€€)

This is a design hotel through and through and each room has its
own theme. The facade is made up of moving coloured-glass slats
that project changing images. Front rooms have lovely views over
the river and the bridges.

✉ Lánchíd utca 19–21, Budapest I ☎ 419 1900; www.lanchid19hotel.hu

Orion Hotel (€€)

Conveniently located at the foot of Castle Hill, this small hotel has
a breakfast room, cocktail lounge and fitness facilities.

✉ Döbrentei utca 13, Budapest I ☎ 356 8583; www.bestwestern.com

Ramada Plaza (€€)

On the Buda river front, with interesting architectural sites
nearby, this large and elegant five-star hotel has rooms with
views across to Margaret Island. It has a large spa and is popular
for conferences.

✉ Árpád fejedelem útja 94, Budapest III ☎ 436 4100;
www.ramadaplazabudapest.com

St George Residence (€€€)

One of the newest of the Castle District hotels, this one is at the
luxury end. The apartments and communal areas are brimming
with character, lavishly decked out with imported furniture and
marble. There is a small restaurant on site.

✉ Fortuna utca 4, Budapest I ☎ 393 5700; www.stgeorgehotelbudapest.co.uk

Victoria (€€)

On the Buda riverbank, this comfortable hotel with full facilities overlooks the old Chain Bridge.

✉ Bem rakpart 11, Budapest I ☎ 457 8080; www.victoria.hu ❓ Rooms on the less scenic side are less expensive.

RESTAURANTS

Alabárdos (€€€)

In one of the most venerable buildings on Castle Hill, this refined establishment offers the best in Hungarian cuisine in an elegant, candlelit setting.

✉ Országház utca 2, Budapest I ☎ 356 0851; www.alabardos.hu
🕐 Mon–Fri 7pm–11pm, Sat 12–4, 7–11

Arany Kaviár (€€)

This restaurant specializes in caviar, but there are a host of other Russian specialities on the menu, and a good wine list.

✉ Ostrom utca 19, Budapest I ☎ 201 6737; www.aranykaviar.hu
🕐 Daily 12–12

Café Pierrot (€€)

Enjoy Hungarian specialities with an international flavour, including a vegetarian menu. There's piano music in the evenings.

✉ Fortuna utca 14, Budapest I ☎ 375 6971; www.pierrot.hu 🕐 Daily 11am–midnight

ICON Restaurant (€€)

This is the restaurant of the Hilton Hotel (➤ 96–97), and its setting in the picturesque Buda Castle District makes it an attractive place to eat if you are in the area. Try to bag a window table.

✉ Hess András tér 1–3, Budapest I ☎ 889 6757; www.iconetterem.hu
🕐 Daily 7–11, 12–3, 6–12

Kacsa (€€)

Duck is the speciality here, but the restaurant also serves other dishes. There's live piano and violin music in the evenings.

✉ Fő utca 75, Budapest I ☎ 201 9992; www.kacsavendeglo.hu 🕐 Daily 12–12

Kéhli (€€)
See page 58.

Kisbuda Gyöngye (€€)
See page 59.

Leroy Cafe (€€)
This is hugely popular with office workers for its quick service, large menu and daily specials. Everything from Indonesian chicken curry to Italian pastas is available.

✉ Bécsi út 63, Budapest III ☎ 439 1698; www.leroycafeobuda.hu
🕐 Daily 11:30am–midnight

Maharaja (€)
Maharaja serves the most authentic Indian cuisine in these parts. Certainly, it's toned down for Hungarian palates, but its rogan josh or korma have enough spice to please all the same. There's another outlet in district VII.

✉ Bécsi út 89–91, Budapest III ☎ 250 7544; www.maharaja.hu
🕐 Daily 12–12

Malomtó (€€–€€€)
See page 59.

Manna Lounge (€€€)
This restaurant has a panoramic terrace directly above the tunnel entrance at the back of the Castle District. The cuisine is a mix of Hungarian, French and Italian; lounge music helps you relax.

✉ Palota út 17, Budapest I ☎ 06 20 999 9188; www.mannalounge.com
🕐 Mon–Sat 12–12

Margitkert (€€)
Margitkert is a traditional Hungarian restaurant a short but steep walk from Margaret Bridge, serving classic, meat-heavy dishes. The highlight is the gypsy band, which plays from around 6pm.

✉ Margit utca 15, Budapest II ☎ 326 0860; www.margitkert.com
🕐 Daily 12–12

Pavillon de Paris (€€)

The recently opened Pavillon sits opposite the French Institute, and appropriately enough specializes in French cuisine. The shady garden makes a romantic spot.

✉ Fő utca 20, Budapest I ☎ 225 0174; www.pavillondeparis.hu

🕐 Tue–Sat 12–12

Rivalda (€€€)

This restaurant has a theatrically inspired decor, hence the name (Front of Stage). The Castle Theatre is next door. There's jazz piano music in the evenings. The broad outdoor eating area in the courtyard of what was once an 18th-century monastery is lovely.

✉ Szinház utca 5–9, Budapest I ☎ 489 0236; www.rivalda.net

🕐 Daily 11:30–11:30

Seoul House (€)

A Korean restaurant, Seoul House serves authentic *kimchee* and excellent beef dishes in a very pleasant and friendly atmosphere.

✉ Fő utca 8, Budapest I ☎ 201 7452 🕐 Mon–Sat 12–11

Symbol (€€)

Symbol has seven separate sections, each offering a different experience. As you walk in, you come to a glass-covered cocktail bar that gives way to a pair of restaurants, a sports bar, a cafe, a music club and an exhibiton hall. It's a full night's entertainment under one roof.

✉ Bécsi út 56, Budapest III ☎ 333 5656; www.symbolbudapest.hu

🕐 Opening hours vary; Italian-fusion restaurant: daily 11:30am–midnight

Szent Jupát (€)

This highly recommended restaurant serves mainly Hungarian dishes from an extensive menu. The huge portions are excellently prepared and cooked, and there is a good selection of beers and wines. Be prepared to share a booth; here you'll find a genial atmosphere and busy staff.

✉ Dékán utca 3, Budapest II ☎ 212 2923; www.stjupat.hu

🕐 Daily 11am–midnight

Új Sipos Halászkert (€€)

The restaurant, in the picturesque, cobbled main square of Old Buda, specializes in a wide selection of river fish from Hungarian lakes and rivers, as well as other Hungarian dishes.

✉ Fő tér 6, Budapest III ☎ 388 8745; www.ujsipos.hu ⏰ Daily 12–12

Vadrózsa (€€€)

Excellent food is served in a small baroque villa, where you can also dine alfresco in a pleasant garden. Specialities include grilled goose liver and a variety of game dishes. Piano music is played as you dine.

✉ Pentelei Molnár utca 15, Budapest II ☎ 326 5817; www.vadrozsa.hu
⏰ Daily 12–3, 7–12

CAFES

Angelika

In the vaulted rectory of Szent Anna templom (➤ 93), Angelika is a suitably respectable cafe that attracts an older clientele happy to sit and chat the day away.

✉ Batthyány tér 7, Budapest I ☎ 225 1653; www.angelikacafe.hu
⏰ Daily 9am–11pm

Auguszt

The Auguszt family have been the proud owners of this patisserie since it first opened back in 1870. With decorative cakes and savoury pastries, you can't go wrong. There are two other outlets in the city.

✉ Fény utca 8, Budapest II ☎ 316 3817; www.augusztcukraszda.hu
⏰ Mon–Fri 10–6, Sat 9–6

Daubner

Daubner has constant queues of eager sweet-toothers waiting for its delectable cakes and pastries despite its poor location far from much of anything. Unfortunately there's nowhere to sit. Its traditional Christmas pastry – called *bejgli* – is delicious.

✉ Szépvölgyi út 50, Budapest II ☎ 335 2253; www.daubnercukraszda.hu
⏰ Daily 9–7

Miró

Attracting a young crowd, the cafe is designed entirely in the spirit of the Catalan artist whose name it celebrates.

✉ Úri utca 30, Budapest I ☎ 201 5573 ⏱ Daily 9am–midnight

Ruszwurm

This is the city's oldest cafe, in the Castle District. Excellent cakes can be eaten here or taken away.

✉ Szentháromság utca 7, Budapest I ☎ 375 5284; www.ruszwurm.hu
⏱ Daily 10–7

SHOPPING

Bortársaság (Wine Society)

Choose from a fine selection of more than 100 wines from Hungarian vintners. There is another outlet in the city, at Lánchíd utca 5.

✉ Batthyány utca 59, Budapest I ☎ 212 0262; www.bortarsasag.hu
⏱ Mon–Fri 10–7, Sat 10–6

Hadik Herend

The celebrated porcelain makers Herend sell their beautiful and elaborate wares close to the centre of Castle Hill.

✉ Szentháromság utca 5, Budapest I ☎ 225 1051; www.herend.com
⏱ Mon–Fri 10–6, Sat 10–2

Herendi Majolika

This place sells Herend "village pottery" and Ajka crystal, ranging from table services to individual pieces.

✉ Bem rakpart 37, Budapest I ☎ 356 7899; www.herendmajolika.hu
⏱ Tue–Fri 9–5, Sat 9–12

House of Royal Wines

This is a wine house and museum in one. Wander around the cellars of the old palace learning about the history of Hungarian wine and then sample and buy wine.

✉ Nyugati sétány, Szent György tér, Budapest I ☎ 267 1100;
www.kiralyiborok.com ⏱ Daily 12–8 (Oct–Apr closed Mon)

Mammut

One of the city's largest shopping malls, Mammut houses high-street names and smaller specialist shops, such as Cigar Shop (tel: 345 8535), which stocks a huge array of cigars, and Budai Borvár (tel: 345 8098), whose wine selection is well above par.

✉ Lövőház utca 2–6, Budapest II ☎ 345 8020; www.mammut.hu
🕐 Mon–Sat 10–9, Sun 10–6

Vinum Primatis

This shop sells wines of the Primatical Wine Guild, whose members act as ambassadors for Hungarian wine.

✉ Úri utca 18, Budapest I ☎ 356 5828; www.vinumprimatis.hu
🕐 Tue–Sun 10–6

ENTERTAINMENT

NIGHTLIFE
Bambi

This bar's interior design is authentically communist, with many of the original 1960s fittings still in place. A gem.

✉ Frankel Leó út 2–4, Budapest I ☎ 212 3171 🕐 Mon–Fri 7am–9pm, Sat–Sun 9–8

Dokk Café

Don't let the name and location mislead you: this is one of the most popular nightclubs in Budapest, playing R'n'B hits from the past and present. In the summer it moves outdoors to Shipyard Island (Dokk Beach).

✉ Mammut shopping centre, Lövőház utca 2–6, Budapest II ☎ 345 8531; www.dokkcafe.hu 🕐 Restaurant: daily 11am–midnight. Club: Thu–Sat 10pm–5am

Jam

Dokk's biggest rival, in the basement of the shopping mall, this club specializes in more cheesy music but is no less popular. It has an outdoor summer club at the northern tip of Margitsziget.

✉ Lövőház utca 1–3, Budapest II ☎ 345 8301; www.jampub.hu
🕐 Mon–Wed 9pm–4am, Thu–Sat 9pm–6am

Lánchíd Söröző

A small and inviting pub in Víziváros, with a retro look.

✉ Fő utca 4, Budapest I ☎ 214 3144; www.lanchidsorozo.hu ⏱ Daily
9am–11pm

LIVE ARTS

International Buda Stage

On the road into the Buda Hills, this small theatre stages both
English- and Hungarian-language plays, films, concerts and dance.

✉ Tárogató út 2-4, Budapest II ☎ 391 2525

Millenáris

This cultural centre houses the Palace of Wonders and the House
of the Future, both interactive exhibitions for children. Concerts,
theatrical shows and dance performances also crop up.

✉ Kis Rókus utca 16–20, Budapest II ☎ 336 4000; www.millenaris.hu
⏱ Opening hours vary. Park daily 6am–11pm

Nemzeti Táncszínház (National Dance Theatre)

On Castle Hill, the National Dance Theatre is the best place to
catch dance in the country. Performances range from classic
ballets to experimental gypsy works.

✉ Színház utca 1–3, Budapest I ☎ 201 4407; www.dancetheatre.hu

Óbudai Társaskör (Óbuda Society)

This small venue in the heart of Óbuda hosts a variety of
performances, from orchestral pieces to Hungarian folk concerts.

✉ Kiskorona utca 7, Budapest III ☎ 250 0288; www.obudaitarsaskor.hu

SPORT

Horse-riding

Hungarians have a tradition of horsemanship and places worth
considering for riding are the Budapest Equestrian Club and the
Petneházy Horse-riding School.

Budapest Equestrian Club ✉ Kerepesi út 7, Budapest VIII ☎ 313 5210
Petneházy Horse-riding School ✉ Feketefej utca, Budapest II
☎ 06 20 567 1616

Gellért-hegy and the Tabán

**Towering over the Danube at a
height of 230m (754ft), Gellért
Hill is hard to miss. Topped with
an impressive monument, it's a
magnet for tourists. The Tabán, on
the other hand, attracts few visitors,
but is a unique corner of the city that
is worth exploring.**

Visitors to lofty Gellért-hegy will find expansive views of
the city, a forbidding 19th-century Citadella, atmospheric
Sziklatemplom (cave church) and a stunning art nouveau
thermal bath, the Gellért Gyógyfürdő (Gellért Thermal Baths).

The Tabán, a small valley squeezed between Gellért-hegy
and Vár-hegy, is today a peaceful, leafy place that was once
home to a large portion of Budapest's 18th- and 19th-century
Serbian population. Only a few buildings remain from this time,
including the Rác Gyógyfürdő (Rác Thermal Baths, ► 67).
Here also is the statue of the beloved Empress Elisabeth,
the quintessential "It girl" of the 19th century.

Gellért-hegy

CITADELLA (CITADEL)

This grim, formidable stronghold on top of Gellért-hegy (Gellért Hill) was built after the Revolution of 1848–49, its principal military purpose to control Castle Hill. Parts of it were symbolically demolished in 1894. It has been a prison camp, accommodation for the homeless, site of an anti-aircraft battery, and, now, a tourist attraction. It's a unique viewing point from which to look down on the city (telescope rental available). At the citadel's eastern end is the Liberation Monument (➤ 109).

www.citadella.hu

🏠 3L 🖂 Citadella sétány, Budapest XI ☎ 365 6076 🍴 Cafe (€€) 🕐 Open access 🚌 Bus: 27. Tram: 18, 19, 47, 49 ❓ 20 Aug: magnificent fireworks on Gellért Hill

GELLÉRT EMLÉKMŰ (GELLÉRT MONUMENT)

Facing the Buda end of Elizabeth Bridge, the monument was erected in 1904, and is one of the ten royal statues donated to the capital by Emperor Franz Joseph. It is especially impressive when floodlit at night. It was from the top of Gellért Hill, where the monument stands, that St Gellért (Gerard), the Bishop of Csanád, was pushed by pagan Hungarians he had come to convert to Christianity. After this ignominious fall, legend tells that he was nailed up in a barrel and thrown unceremoniously into the Danube.

🏠 4K 🖂 Gellért-hegy, Budapest XI 🕐 Open access 🍴 Panorama Restaurant (€€, ➤ 114) 🚌 Bus: 27. Tram: 18, 19

GELLÉRT-HEGY

Best places to see, ➤ 38–39.

HOTEL GELLÉRT ÉS GELLÉRT GYÓGYFÜRDŐ (GELLÉRT HOTEL AND GELLÉRT THERMAL BATHS)

Described by a local illustrator as a "huge white gem", the Danubius Gellért Hotel (to give it its full name) is one of the most prestigious in Budapest. The hotel, along with its thermal baths, was built as part of a civic policy to make Budapest into a city of baths. If not taking a dip, then have a look at the mosaic floor and glass ceiling. From the back of the hall you can see into the roofed part of the swimming pool. Also see the outdoor pool, its polished postmodern lines contrasting with the bulky art nouveau building, which was completed in 1918. The outdoor pool stretches to the other side of Kemenes utca and is connected to the main area by a subway. If you're not feeling energetic, you can relax with an ice cream or a beer on the terrace.

www.budapestgyogyfurdoi.hu

🔡 4M ✉ Hotel: Szent Gellért tér 1, Budapest XI. Thermal baths: Kelenhegyi út, Budapest XI ☎ Hotel: 889 5500. Thermal baths: 466 6166 ✋ Baths: free if a resident of the hotel, otherwise expensive 🍴 Panorama Restaurant (€€, ➤ 114) 🚌 Bus: 7, 86. Tram: 18, 19, 47, 49

SZABADSÁG HÍD (FREEDOM BRIDGE)

This masterpiece of aesthetic engineering was opened in 1896 as part of the millennium celebrations, when Emperor Franz Joseph himself hammered in the final rivet. "When designing the bridge," said its architect, Virgil Nagy, "I had to obey the requirements

of beauty, simplicity and economy". On top of each pillar, surmounting a golden ball, is a Turul, Hungary's mythical bird.

✚ 5L ✉ Szent Gellért tér, Budapest XI, to Fővám tér, Budapest IX
🍴 Panorama Restaurant (€€, ➤ 114) 🚌 Bus: 7, 86. Tram: 18, 19, 47, 49

SZABADSÁG SZOBOR (LIBERATION MONUMENT)

Situated by the Citadella as a sombre reminder of Budapest's more recent turbulent past, the Liberation, or Freedom, Monument commemorates the Soviet-led liberation of the city from the Germans in 1945. Originally intended to honour the dictator Admiral Horthy's son (a young pilot who died in a crash believed to have been engineered by the Germans), the monument was adapted by the communists to reflect a new era, with the addition of a soldier figure and the inscription: "To the liberating Soviet heroes from a grateful Hungarian people". However, few Hungarians who lived through that time shared the sentiment, and the monument has been adapted again with the removal of the soldier.

✚ 4L ✉ Citadella sétány, Budapest XI ☎ 175 6451 🕓 Open access
🍴 Aranyszarvas (€€, ➤ 113) 🚌 Bus: 27. Tram: 18, 19

SZIKLATEMPLOM (CAVE CHURCH)

The unusual Sziklatemplom overlooks the Danube opposite Gellért Hotel on the hill's southern side. Built by the Pauline order in 1931, it was closed in the early 1950s by the communists, who immediately bordered up the entranceway and jailed the monks. It reopened in 1990 and has been in use since 1992. The interior is warm and comfortable, with tiled flooring, plants, stained-glass windows and natural cave walls; religious ornaments are surprisingly few. Note the slab of concrete to the right of the church entrance as you enter – it's the last remnant of the wall that once closed in the church.

✚ 4L ✉ Gellért-hegy, Budapest XI ☎ 385 1529 🕓 Daily 9–9 ✋ Free
🍴 Panorama Restaurant (€€, ➤ 114) 🚌 Bus: 7, 86. Tram: 18, 19, 41, 47, 49

The Tabán

ERZSÉBET KIRÁLYNÉ SZOBOR (STATUE OF QUEEN ELISABETH)

This statue honours Elisabeth (1837–98), wife of Habsburg Emperor Franz Joseph. Descended from Bavarian aristocrats, the beautiful Elisabeth (or "Sissi" as she was fondly known) was one of the few members of the ruling dynasty to win the affections of Hungarians. Estranged from her husband, Sissi met an untimely end at the hands of an assassin on the banks of Lake Geneva.

🚇 4K ✉ Döbrentei tér, Budapest I 🚌 Tram: 18, 19

RUDAS GYÓGYFÜRDŐ (RUDAS THERMAL BATHS)

The first thermal baths built on the site of Rudas date from the 14th century, but the current incarnation, which has had a thorough renovation, was constructed by the Turks in 1566. It is arguably the most Turkish of all Budapest's baths, and a soak in its domed octagonal room, particularly when the sun pierces the roof's small windows, is not only a soothing experience but also a trip back in time. The Turkish baths are men-only on Monday and

Wednesday to Friday; Tuesday is women only. On weekends it's mixed but swimwear is required. The swimming pool wing, dating from the late 1800s, is neoclassical in style and has mixed bathing throughout the week.

www.budapestgyogyfurdoi.hu

🚇 4K ✉ Döbrentei tér 9, Budapest I
☎ 356 1322 🕐 Swimming pool: Mon–Wed 6–6, Thu, Sun 6am–8pm, Fri–Sat 6am–8pm, 10pm–4am. Baths: Sun–Thu 6am–8pm, Fri–Sat 6am–8pm, 10pm–4am. 💶 Expensive
🚌 Bus: 7. Tram: 18, 19

SEMMELWEIS ORVOSTÖRTÉNETI MÚZEUM (MUSEUM OF MEDICAL HISTORY)

Semmelweis is one of the more intriguing yet overlooked museums in the city. It documents the history of medicine from early tribal practices to the beginning of the 20th century through a vast array of highly unusual artefacts, including a mummified human head and falcon from Egypt. Wax models of human organs are incredibly detailed, while the tools of surgery from the 16th to 19th centuries look particularly nasty. One room contains the reconstructed Holy Ghost Pharmacy, founded in 1786, while another contains a 19th-century dentist's chair that would be perfect for a horror flick. The museum is named after Ignác Semmelweis, the doctor who discovered the cause of puerperal fever. Known as the "saviour of mothers", he realized doctors needed to sterilize their hands, clothes and instruments between autopsies and assisting with births. He was born in the house and is buried in its garden.

www.semmelweis.museum.hu

✚ 3K ✉ Apród utca 1–3, Budapest I ☎ 375 3333 ⚙ Mid-Mar to Oct Tue–Sun 10:30–6; Nov to mid-Mar Tue–Sun 10:30–4 💰 Inexpensive
🚌 Tram: 19

SZARVAS-HÁZ (DEER HOUSE)

This triangular-shaped cafe was built at the beginning of the 19th century in late rococo style. Famous for its game dishes, it's now the Aranyszarvas Restaurant (➤ 113). The Deer House was once part of the Tabán, a popular place of entertainment on the northern slope of Gellért Hill. Many of the houses here, apart from the Deer House, were demolished for public health reasons. All the more reason to eat at the Deer House, which is scrupulously clean.

www.aranyszarvas.hu

✚ 3K ✉ Szarvas tér, Budapest I ☎ 375 6451 ⚙ Daily 12–11
🚌 Bus: 16, 78. Tram: 19

HOTELS

Ábel Panzió (€)

This small but comfortable villa, fully refurbished with antique furniture, is in a quiet area just southwest of the Citadel. It's the perfect place to escape the hustle and bustle of the city.

✉ Ábel Jenő utca 9, Budapest XI ☎ 209 2537; www.abelpanzio.hu

Danubius Hotel Flamenco (€€€)

This is a large hotel, just south of Gellért Hill and a few minutes from the business and shopping areas. It offers a wide range of facilities: a restaurant (with a summer terrace), bars, live music, car rental, a business centre and full leisure facilities.

✉ Tas vezér utca 3–7, Budapest XI ☎ 889 5600; www.danubiushotels.com

Danubius Hotel Gellért (€€)

This four-star art nouveau hotel (➤ 107) is one of Budapest's classics, and sits next to the famous Gellért Baths (which hotel guests can access free of charge). Front-facing rooms offer views over the river, as does the splendid Panorama Restaurant (➤ 114).

✉ Szent Gellért tér 1, Budapest XI ☎ 889 5500; www.danubiushotels.com

Hotel Citadella (€)

Hotel Citadella is an inexpensive option for those who aren't afraid of a climb. The hotel sits on top of Gellért Hill, beside the Citadel. The rooms are spacious and clean, if somewhat basic, and there's free parking. The views are excellent.

✉ Citadella sétány, Budapest XI ☎ 466 5794; www.citadella.hu

RESTAURANTS

Aranyszarvas (€€)

Located in the Deer House (➤ 112), Aranyszarvas is a well-established restaurant that's been serving guests for many years. Its solid Hungarian menu follows the seasons, although game, the restaurant's forte, is ever-present – choices include wild boar, stag, venison, pheasant and hare.

✉ Szarvas tér 1, Budapest I ☎ 375 6451; www.aranyszarvas.hu
🕐 Daily 12–11

Búsuló Juhász (€€)

On the northern slopes of Gellért Hill, this trendy restaurant offers panoramic views over the Buda Hills.

✉ Kelenhegyi út 58, Budapest XI ☎ 209 1649; www.busulojuhasz.hu
🕐 Daily 12–12

Panorama Restaurant (€€)

The famous Gellért Hotel's restaurant offers views of the Danube that are as appetizing as the food. Pikeperch dishes and veal Gellért-style are among the many specialities on the menu.

✉ Gellért tér 1, Budapest XI ☎ 889 5550 🕐 Tue–Sat 7pm–midnight, Sun noon–3pm

Tabáni Terasz (€€)

The tastefully renovated 250-year-old house and protected inner courtyard are reasons enough to dine at Tabáni. The international menu features some delectable dishes. Fish is a speciality.

✉ Apród utca 10, Budapest I ☎ 201 1086; www.tabaniterasz.hu
🕐 Daily 12–12

ENTERTAINMENT

A38

Moored by the Buda end of Petőfi Bridge, this Ukrainian cargo boat is now a hip venue, with dancing, concerts, bars and a restaurant.

✉ Műegyetem rakpart, Budapest XI ☎ 464 3940; www.a38.hu

Fonó Budai Zeneház (Fonó Buda Music House)

Fonó is the centre of Hungarian folk and world music in Budapest. It has traditional bands at 8pm on Wednesday and Friday, and Saturday is sometimes graced with bigger, international acts.

✉ Sztregova utca 3, Budapest XI ☎ 206 5300; www.fono.hu

Rio

Alfresco clubs come and go, but Rio has been running for years. It has a Brazilian theme, with palm trees welcoming revellers.

✉ Goldmann György tér, Budapest XII (at the foot of Petőfi Bridge)
☎ 06 30 297 2158; www.rio.hu 🕐 Apr–Sep daily 6pm–5am

Belváros and Lipótváros

For centuries Belváros *was* Pest – nothing existed outside its medieval walls. Nowadays it is the heart of Budapest on the east side of the Danube and filled with exclusive boutiques and gorgeous art nouveau architecture. But some of the city's most celebrated architecture can also be found in Lipótváros, the business centre that occupies the northern half of the fifth district.

LIPÓTVÁROS

BELVÁROS

Stretching through Belváros is the pedestrian boulevard Váci utca, alive with tourists searching for holiday gifts or the latest fashions. Further north, in Lipótváros, you'll find enormous squares and some exceptional examples of Budapest's celebrated architectural styles, including the neoclassical Országház (Parliament, ➤ 48–49) and Szent István Bazilika (St Stephen's Basilica, ➤ 50–51), and the art nouveau Gresham Palace (➤ 122–123) and Magyar Királyi Takarékpénztár (Former Royal Post Office Savings Bank, ➤ 123).

Belváros

BELVÁROSI PLÉBÁNIATEMPLOM (INNER CITY PARISH CHURCH)

This beautiful church is one of the oldest in the city and is situated uncomfortably close to Elisabeth Bridge on Március 15 tér. The area was once the centre of the fourth-century Roman settlement of Contra-Aquincum and a small display of its remains can be seen close by. Dating from the 12th century, the church was rebuilt in the 18th century after a devastating fire, hence the baroque facade

and interior. At one time the Turks converted it into a mosque and you can still see a Muslim prayer niche or mihrab to the right of the high altar. If you can bear the flyover with all its traffic, delight in the beauty of this church and curse the city planners.

www.belvarosiplebania.hu

➕ 4K ✉ Március 15 tér, Budapest V ☎ 318 3108 🕔 Daily 9–7 ✋ Free 🚇 M3 Ferenciek tér 🚋 Tram: 2

DUNAKORZÓ (DANUBE PROMENADE)

In the latter years of the 19th century much of neoclassical Pest was hidden by large hotels, some the finest and most fashionable in Europe – the Carlton, Ritz, Hungaria and Bristol. This is where the rich and fashionable strolled during the summer, a tradition that had survived from the time when Pest was a small town. It was especially beautiful in the evening, with brightly lit cafes and jazz and gypsy music. Now, with new hotels in the area, the promenade has come to life again, not least because of its magnificent view across the great river to Castle Hill.

➕ 4J ✉ Vigadó tér, Budapest V 🍴 Gerbeaud (€€, ➤ 130) 🚋 Tram: 2

FÖLDALATTI VASÚTI MÚZEUM
(UNDERGROUND RAILWAY MUSEUM)

Hidden away in the Metro station underpass on Deák tér, this tiny, exquisite museum occupies one of the original railway tunnels. It has a fascinating array of plans, models and carriages, and shows the development of the first underground system on the European mainland. The first line, completed in 1896, ran the length of Andrássy út, a distance of 2.3km (1.5 miles). The museum is definitely worth a visit if you're an eager trainspotter. Even if you're not a train fanatic, keep it in mind for a rainy day.

www.bkv.hu

➕ 5J ✉ Deák tér, Budapest V ☎ 461 6500 🕐 Daily 10–5 💷 Inexpensive
🚇 M1/2/3 Deák tér 🚌 Bus: 9, 16, 105. Tram: 47, 49

MAGYAR KERESKEDELMI ÉS
VENDÉGLÁTÓIPARI MÚZEUM
(HUNGARIAN MUSEUM OF
TOURISM AND TRADE)

Hungary's museum of tourism and trade focuses its attention – strangely, considering its name – on the world of catering and commerce. Its commerce section has displays of store signs, promotional material, product packaging and accounting books, but most visitors will find the catering wing more engaging. Here, the large collection of cooking utensils and moulds will make most amateur chefs weep, and the plethora of restaurant menus is impressive. The reconstructed 19th-century cake shop is also a must for any dessert-lover.

www.mkvm.hu

➕ 5H ✉ Szent István tér 15, Budapest V ☎ 375 6249 🕐 Wed–Mon 11–7
💷 Moderate 🍴 Café Kör (€€, ➤ 58) 🚇 M1 Bajcsy-Zsilinszky út,
M2 Arany János utca

VÖRÖSMARTY TÉR (VÖRÖSMARTY SQUARE) AND VÁCI UTCA (VÁCI STREET)

Named after the 19th-century Romantic poet Mihály Vörösmarty (1800–55), the square is a real delight. The poet's monument stands in the centre. On the north side, at No 7, is the famous Gerbeaud cafe (➤ 130). Váci utca, on the far side of the square, is Budapest's premier shopping street. The shopping here is small scale with big brand names – Estée Lauder, Adidas and the like. The entire street is pedestrianized but, attractive as it is, it looks much like any European pedestrianized shopping area.

✚ 4J ✉ Budapest V 🍴 Onyx (€), Vörösmarty tér 7–8; Tue–Sat 12–2:30, 6:30–11 🚇 M1 Vörösmarty tér 🚊 Tram: 2

a walk in the Inner City

This walk in downtown Pest serves as an introduction to the commercial and cultural heart of the city.

Start at Kossuth Lajos tér outside the magnificent Parliament (► 48–49). With your back to the Parliament, turn right down Nádor utca towards Szabadság tér, a hidden gem of the city.

At Nos 8–9 is the stately bulk of the Hungarian National Bank. On the southwest corner towards the square is the figure of Hamlet holding poor Yorick's skull.

Return to Nádor utca and turn right towards József Attila utca. Before reaching it, turn right into Roosevelt tér.

At the northern end is the Hungarian Academy of Sciences (► 123), the first neo-Renaissance building in the city, built between 1862 and 1864. Also on the square is Gresham Palace (► 122), a richly ornate art nouveau building.

Back on Nádor utca, turn right. You come to the intersection with József Attila utca, with its incessant flow of traffic. Cross it and head straight on to József nádor tér, which, before the advent of the automobile, was one of the most attractive squares in the city.

Occupying the square is the Romantic-style Postabank Headquarters; Gross House, a neoclassical apartment building; and the Central European University, a classical chef-d'oeuvre.

Leave József nádor tér and make for Bécsi utca. Turn right, and walk down to Vörösmarty tér (➤ 119), a pleasant and restful square.

At No 7 is the famous Gerbeaud cafe (➤ 130) – so stop for a snack.

Walk to the far side to Váci utca (➤ 119), the most stylish shopping street in town. If you can resist the shops, continue under the subway towards the Central Market Hall on Vámház körút.

The 19th-century market hall (➤ 165) is a place to wander or have a snack or beer at one of the small upstairs bars.

Distance Approximately 3km (2 miles)
Time 2 hours, half a day with stops
Start point Kossuth Lajos tér ✚ 4F 🚇 M2 Kossuth Lajos tér
End point Central Market Hall (Vásárcsarnok) ✚ 5L
🚋 Tram: 2, 2/A, 47, 49. Trolleybus: 83
Lunch Fatál (€, ➤ 58)

Lipótváros

GRESHAM PALACE

Gresham Palace began life as a luxury apartment building/office space of the London-based Gresham Life Insurance Company in 1907. The company commissioned Zsigmond Quittner to deliver the goods, who in turn hired builders József and László Vágó. The open purse and artistic freedom afforded by Gresham allowed Quittner to create a lavish art nouveau design and install the latest technological advances, such as central heating and a dust extraction system. By the end of World War II, however, the palace was in a sorry state, its facade scarred by bomb blasts and its interior ruined by Soviet soldiers. During the communist era the palace was converted into cheap apartments and shops, but in

1998 developers bought the dilapidated building with the intention of turning the historical landmark into a luxury hotel (Four Seasons Hotel, ➤ 126). After a makeover costing US$110 million, the Gresham is once again the pride of Budapest. The T-shaped arcade is restored as a resplendent work of art, topped by a glazed roof, floored with tiled mosaics, and walled with colourful Zsolnay ceramics. The original wrought-iron gate, with its peacock motifs, marks the entrance, and a stained-glass window by Miksa Róth featuring Lajos Kossuth complements the second-floor staircase.
www.fourseasons.com/budapest

✚ 4H ✉ Roosevelt tér 5–6, Budapest V ☎ 268 6000 ♿ Lobby, restaurant and cafe are open to non-guests 🍴 Gresham Café (€€€, ➤ 130) 🚊 Tram: 2

MAGYAR KIRÁLYI POSTA TAKARÉKPÉNZTÁR (FORMER ROYAL POST OFFICE SAVINGS BANK)

Designed by Ödön Lechner in 1900, the Post Office Savings Bank is an exceptional example of Hungarian art nouveau. The facade is a fantastical mix of secessionist styles and Hungarian folk art motifs – look for the swarms of bees climbing the walls to beehives, representative of thrift and saving. The majesty of the lime-green roof is hard to see from street level, but what can be seen of its vibrant Zsolnay tiles and flourishes of yellow trimming is truly captivating. Unfortunately the interior is closed to the public (the building now belongs to the National Bank) and can only be visited one day in May – phone for details. It is, however, possible to take a peek at the Cashiers' Hall during normal working hours.

✚ 4G ✉ Hold utca 4 ☎ 428 2600 🍴 Farger Café (€, ➤ 130) Ⓜ M3 Arany János utca

MAGYAR TUDOMÁNYOS AKADÉMIA (HUNGARIAN ACADEMY OF SCIENCES)

This austere neo-Renaissance building on the northern side of Roosevelt tér was built in 1865 by Friedrich Stüler to house Hungary's Academy of Sciences. The academy was founded 40

years earlier by Count István Széchenyi, who gifted one year's income for the establishment of an institution to explore Hungarian science, arts, literature and language. The act is captured in a bronze relief facing Akadémia utca. Statues of seminal figures from various fields of science also grace the facade: look for Newton, Galileo, Révay, Descartes and Leibnitz.
www.mta.hu

🕂 4H ✉ Roosevelt tér, Budapest V 🎨 Art gallery: Mon, Fri 11–4
🍴 Lou Lou (€€, ➤ 128) 🚋 Tram: 2

NÉPRAJZI MÚZEUM (MUSEUM OF ETHNOGRAPHY)
Strongly resembling Berlin's Reichstag, but much more elegant, this neo-Renaissance palace was built to house the Supreme Court and the Chief Public Prosecutor's Office. Sculptures of legislators, magistrates and goddesses of justice adorn the facade of this large and imposing building. Its grandiose entrance hall features a marble stairway, huge chandeliers and on the ceiling a

splendid fresco by Károly Lotz. Again, this is worth visiting if only for its magnificent architecture and decor. Permanent exhibitions feature ethnological material from across Hungary, including traditional folk costumes, simple farming implements and household items with touches of folk design, painted pottery and furniture, and a reconstructed church from the 18th century.

www.neprajz.hu

🚹 4F 🖂 Kossuth Lajos tér 12, Budapest V ☎ 473 2400 🕓 Tue–Sun 10–6
🖐 Moderate 🍴 Cafe (€) Ⓜ M2 Kossuth Lajos tér 🚌 Bus: 15. Tram: 2.
Trolleybus: 70, 78

ORSZÁGHÁZ (PARLIAMENT)

Best places to see, ➤ 48–49.

SZABADSÁG TÉR (LIBERTY SQUARE)

This vast open space in the city centre between the Parliament building and St Stephen's Basilica was laid out by Antal Palóczy in 1902. The site was once occupied by a huge military barracks and prison where many a Hungarian patriot was incarcerated. Among the different palaces, one art nouveau building, the American Embassy, is very prominent. The statue in front of the building is of the US General Harry Hill Bandholtz. An officer of the Allied peace-keeping force in 1919, he saved the treasures of the National Museum by sealing its doors. The seals bore the US coat of arms and so deterred the soldiers of the occupying Romanian army from plundering the museum. Also on the square and nearby are the headquarters of Hungarian television, the Ministry of Agriculture, the Ethnographical Museum and the Post Office Savings Bank.

🚹 4G 🖂 Budapest V 🍴 Farger Café (€, ➤ 130) Ⓜ M2 Kossuth Lajos tér
🚌 Bus: 15. Tram: 2

SZENT ISTVÁN BAZILIKA (ST STEPHEN'S BASILICA)

Best places to see, ➤ 50–51.

HOTELS

Astoria (€€)

Sumptuously splendid with a *fin-de-siècle* atmosphere, but there is nothing remotely stuffy about this four-star hotel; it is relaxing and unhurried and its elegant restaurant-cafe (► 128) is popular.

✉ Kossuth Lajos utca 19–21, Budapest V ☎ 889 6000; www.danubiushotels.com

City Hotel Mátyás (€)

One of Pest's central, good-value options. Rooms are fairly unexciting, but they're more than adequate.

✉ Március 15 tér 7–8, Budapest V ☎ 338 4711; www.cityhotelmatyas.hu

Four Seasons Hotel (€€€)

One of the city's landmark buildings, the magnificent art nouveau Gresham Palace (► 122) dominates Roosevelt Square at the Pest end of the Chain Bridge. Immaculately restored, it houses what is arguably the city's top hotel, the five-star Four Seasons.

✉ Roosevelt tér 5–6, Budapest V ☎ 268 6000; www.fourseasons.com

Hotel Art (€€)

In a side street in the heart of Old Pest, this large, three-star hotel has won awards for its original architecture. It has comfortable modern rooms and a restaurant with Transylvanian specialities.

✉ Király Pál utca 12, Budapest V ☎ 266 2166; www.bestwestern.com

Hotel Parlament (€€)

This is a well-placed hotel, a hundred yards from Parliament. Rooms are minimalist and modern and the lobby bar offers free tea/coffee and pastries between 10 and 5.

✉ Kálmán Imre utca 19, Budapest V ☎ 374 6000; www.parlament-hotel.hu

Kempinski Hotel Corvinus (€€€)

This striking, postmodern hotel has three elegant facades and one plain one. Its rooms are immaculate and it has a couple of excellent restaurants.

✉ Erzsébet tér 7–8, Budapest V ☎ 429 3777; www.kempinski-budapest.com

Leo Panzió (€)

With Váci utca only one block from its front door, Leo is about as central as it gets. Rooms have a dated look but they're quite comfortable and fitted with air conditioning for summer days.

✉ Kossuth Lajos utca 2/A, Budapest V ☎ 266 9041; www.leopanzio.hu

Le Meridien Budapest (€€€)

In an elegant building that is a declared historic monument, this luxurious hotel has rooms decorated with period furniture and chandeliers. A beautiful atrium, with a stained-glass dome, is the setting for Le Bourbon restaurant.

✉ Erzsébet tér 9–10, Budapest V ☎ 429 5500; www.lemeridienbudapest.com

Sofitel Promenade Budapest (€€€)

This hotel and conference centre, on the bank of the Danube, is suave, efficient, comfortable and has all the modern conveniences you would expect to find in a top-class hotel. Its restaurant, the Paris Budapest Café, serves French and Hungarian fusion dishes.

✉ Roosevelt tér 2, Budapest V ☎ 266 1234; www.sofitel.com/budapest

Starlight Suites (€€€)

These contemporary suites have leather chairs and gleaming, tiled bathrooms. Service is prompt and professional, and, in the heart of Belváros, it's hard to find a more central location.

✉ Mérleg utca 6, Budapest V ☎ 484 3700; www.starlighthotels.com

RESTAURANTS

Café Kör (€€)

See page 58.

Cyrano (€€)

With its finely designed interior, this is a favourite of the Budapest business community. It offers a good menu, with a selection of reasonably priced wines. The restaurant prides itself on being a location for the filming of *Cyrano de Bergerac*.

✉ Kristóf tér, Budapest V ☎ 266 4747; www.cyranorestaurant.info 🕐 Daily 8am–midnight

Fatál (€)

See page 58.

Govinda (€)

Govinda serves fresh vegetarian and vegan Indian cuisine, including polenta-based dishes, vegetable rice, dhal and soups. Its cellar location is cool in summer and warm in winter and service is very friendly.

✉ Vigyázó Ferenc utca 4, Budapest V ☎ 269 1625; www.govinda.hu
🕐 Mon–Fri 11:30–8, Sat–Sun 12–8

Kárpátia (€€€)

Kárpátia's richly painted vaulted ceilings and walls are reminiscent of Mátyás-templom (➤ 46–47), as are its stained-glass windows. The menu of Hungarian and Transylvanian specialities is small but selective, and there's accompanying gypsy music most nights.

✉ Ferenciek tere 7–8, Budapest V ☎ 317 3596; www.karpatia.hu
🕐 Daily 11–11

Lou Lou (€€)

This excellent French restaurant with Hungarian appeal offers a good choice of wines, beers and spirits.

✉ Vigyázó Ferenc utca 4, Budapest V ☎ 312 4505;
www.loulourestaurant.com 🕐 Mon–Fri 12–3, 7–11, Sat 7–11

Mirror Café Restaurant (€€)

This very plush restaurant is in the impressive Astoria Hotel (➤ 126). Elegant surroundings complement the high standards of Hungarian and international fare.

✉ Kossuth Lajos utca 19–21, Budapest V ☎ 889 6000 🕐 Daily 7am–11pm

Óceán Bár & Grill (€€–€€€)

Serving fresh fish flown in from Scandinavia daily, Óceán is leagues ahead of most other fish restaurants in Budapest. The interior has a fresh, clean look (aquarium included, of course), with big windows overlooking the river.

✉ Petőfi tér 3, Budapest V ☎ 266 1826 🕐 Daily 12–12

Ruben (€€)

This great-value restaurant, a few minutes' walk from Astoria station, serves Hungarian dishes and has an extensive wine list.

✉ Magyar utca 12–14, Budapest V ☎ 266 3649; www.rubenrestaurant.hu
🕐 Daily 12–12

Spoon (€€–€€€)

Spoon is one of a string of boat-restaurants on the Danube with views of Buda. It stands out for its superb Hungarian wines and international menu, which also caters for vegetarians and children.

✉ Vigadó tér 3, Budapest V ☎ 411 0933; www.spooncafe.hu 🕐 Daily 12–12

Taverna Dionysos (€)

On Pest Quay, with an interior like a Hellenic village square, this restaurant is located in attractive surroundings and serves a good choice of excellent Greek dishes.

✉ Belgrád rakpart 16, Budapest V ☎ 318 1222; www.dionysos.hu
🕐 Daily 12–12

Trattoria Pomo d'Oro (€€€)

This restaurant, near Roosevelt tér, has a menu focusing on tomato – hence the name. Pasta and pizza play the central role.

✉ Arany János utca 9, Budapest V ☎ 302 6473;
www.pomodorobudapest.com 🕐 Daily 12–12 ❓ Reservations advised

CAFES

Café Alibi

A neat, unpretentious cafe, Alibi attracts a mainly female crowd with its quiet ambience, strong coffee and rich hot chocolate.

✉ Egyetem tér 4, Budapest V ☎ 317 4209; www.cafealibi.hu 🕐 Mon–Wed 8am–9pm, Thu–Fri 8am–10pm, Sat 9–9, Sun 9–5

Central Kávéház

An archetypal Budapest coffee house that has been lovingly restored. Enjoy dinner or indulge in coffee and succulent cakes.

✉ Károly Mihály utca 9, Budapest V ☎ 266 2110; www.centralkavehaz.hu
🕐 Mon–Fri 8am–11pm

Farger Café

A modern cafe that's hugely popular with laptop owners looking for free wireless connection over breakfast or a long, drawn-out coffee. Children are heartily welcomed and the best window seats overlooking Szabadság tér normally fill up first.

✉ Zoltán utca 18, Budapest V ☎ 06 20 237 7825; www.farger.hu
🕐 Mon–Fri 7am–10pm, Sat–Sun 9–5

Gerbeaud

Another venerable city institution, Gerbeaud has been here since 1870. The cafe serves a fine selection of pastries and there is now a restaurant and beer hall with its own micro-brewery.

✉ Vörösmary tér 7, Budapest V ☎ 429 9000; www.gerbeaud.hu 🕐 Daily 9–9

Gerlóczy

Serving breakfast, lunch and dinner, along with excellent cakes and coffee, this cafe is a favourite with locals. Its Parisian charm is reinforced by the tables set on the square in the shade of an oak.

✉ Kamermayer Károly tér, Budapest V ☎ 501 4000; www.gerloczy.hu
🕐 Daily 7am–11pm

Gresham Café

Gresham recalls the heady days of the 1920s when the Gresham Circle, a group of Budapest's literary elite, met here to exchange ideas and broaden minds. Its lovingly reconstructed art deco interior is a perfect complement to the rest of the palace (➤ 122). It's now part of the Four Seasons Hotel (➤ 126).

✉ Roosevelt tér 5–6, Budapest V ☎ 268 6000; www.fourseasons.com
🕐 Mon–Wed 6:30–11, 12–10, Thu–Sat 6:30–11, 12–10:30, Sun 7–11, 12–10

SHOPPING

ANTIQUES AND ART

Bardoni

This gallery has a good selection of 20th-century furniture and other items. The emphasis here is on art deco.

✉ Falk Miksa utca 12, Budapest V ☎ 269 0090; www.bardoni.hu
🕐 Tue–Sat 10–6

BÁV

Bizományi Áruhaz Vállalat (BÁV), the state-owned chain, offers one of the best chances to pick up a bargain. The outlets sell paintings, jewellery, carpets, porcelain, rugs and furnishings.

✉ Bécsi utca 1–3, Budapest V ☎ 429 3020; www.bav.hu ⏰ Mon–Fri 10–6, Sat 10–4 ❓ This is one of many branches

Csók István Gallery

Certainly one of the best galleries for contemporary Hungarian art.

✉ Váci utca 25, Budapest V ☎ 318 5826 ⏰ Mon–Fri 10–8, Sat 10–1

Ernst Gallery

The gallery exhibits early 20th-century Hungarian art and furniture, including ceramics, paintings, sculptures and carpets. There's another outlet in nearby Zrínyi utca.

✉ Irányi utca 27, Budapest V ☎ 266 4016; www.ernstgaleria.hu ⏰ Mon–Fri 10:30–6:30, Sat 10–2

Haas Galéria

It's worth going up the dimly lit steps and across the gloomy courtyard to find this intimate gallery specializing in the little-known Hungarian contribution to 20th-century avant-garde art.

✉ Falk Miksa utca 13, Budapest V ☎ 302 5337; www.haasgaleria.hu ⏰ Mon–Fri 10–6, Sat 10–1

Kieselbach Galéria

The leading venue for (mostly 20th-century) Hungarian art. There are exhibitions and auctions – indeed, the gallery holds the record for the most expensive piece of Hungarian art ever sold.

✉ Szent István körút 5, Budapest V ☎ 269 3148; www.kieselbach.hu ⏰ Mon–Fri 10–6, Sat 10–1

Magma

Showcases the latest Hungarian designers and their work, which ranges from porcelain and jewellery to furniture and paintings.

✉ Petőfi Sándor utca 11, Budapest V ☎ 235 0277; www.magma.hu ⏰ Mon–Fri 10–7, Sat 10–3

Millennium Antik

This store has a wonderful array of antiques and specializes in antique linens, dresses, shawls, dolls and jewellery.

✉ Váci utca 67, Budapest V ☎ 318 1478; www.millennium-antik.hu
🕐 Mon–Fri 10–6, Sat 10–2

Montparnasse

Museum-quality, mostly French, restored art deco furniture, including display cabinets, lights, mirrors and sideboards.

✉ Falk Miksa utca 10, Budapest V ☎ 302 6444; www.montparnasse.co.uk
🕐 Mon–Fri 10–6, Sat 10–2

Pintér Antik

For more than 20 years this shop has specialized in furniture and chandeliers, as well as smaller items like jewellery and silverware.

✉ Falk Miksa utca 10, Budapest V ☎ 311 3030; www.pinterantik.hu
🕐 Mon–Fri 10–6, Sat 10–2

Polgár Gallery

This gallery and auction house specializes largely in paintings, with some furniture and jewellery. It holds four auctions a year. There's a larger outlet, focusing more on furniture, at Váci utca 11/b.

✉ Kossuth Lajos utca 3, Budapest V ☎ 317 3013; www.polgar-galeria.hu
🕐 Mon–Fri 10–6, Sat 10–1

Virág Judit Gallery

Exhibitions of 19th- and 20th-century Hungarian paintings and Zsolnay porcelain are held here. There are three auctions a year.

✉ Falk Miksa utca 30, Budapest V ☎ 312 2071; www.viragjuditgaleria.hu
🕐 Mon–Fri 10–6, Sat 10–1

BOOKS
Bestsellers

This store sells a wide range of fiction and non-fiction, magazines and guides. It's the best English-language bookshop in the city.

✉ Október 6 utca 11, Budapest V ☎ 312 1295; www.bestsellers.hu
🕐 Mon–Fri 9–6:30, Sat 10–5, Sun 10–4

Központi Antikvárium

The Central Antiquarian Bookshop, established in 1881, has a huge selection of maps and foreign books.

✉ Múzeum körút 13–15, Budapest V ☎ 317 3514 🕐 Mon–Fri 10–6:30, Sat 10–2

Libri Stúdium

There's a good selection of foreign-language books in this central branch of a leading chain of booksellers. Other well-stocked outlets, with cafes, are at Rákóczi út 12 and in the Mammut mall.

✉ Váci utca 22, Budapest V ☎ 318 5680; www.libri.hu 🕐 Mon–Fri 10–7, Sat–Sun 10–3

Nyugat Antikvárium

The shelves of rare foreign-language books, prints and maps here will keep you browsing for hours.

✉ Bajcsy-Zsilinszky út 34, Budapest V ☎ 311 9023 🕐 Mon–Fri 10–5:30

FASHION
Bershka

The international chain opened its first shop in Hungary on the site once occupied by the Luxus department store, the largest of its kind in the communist era. It sells men's and women's fashion.

✉ Vörösmarty tér 3, Budapest V ☎ 411 1802; www.bershka.com
🕐 Mon–Sat 10–7, Sun 11–5

Carum Carvi Fashion House

If you want a made-to-measure suit, try here. The store also does off-the-peg clothes, for men and women.

✉ Kossuth Lajos utca 17, Budapest V 🕐 Mon–Fri 10–6, Sat 10–1

Salamander

With three outlets on Váci utca alone, Salamander sells major international footwear brands, such as Lacoste, Tommy Hilfiger and Timberland.

✉ Váci utca 23, Budapest V ☎ 434 5575; www.salamander.de 🕐 Mon–Fri 10–7, Sat 10–5, Sun 11–5

FOOD AND DRINK
La Boutique des Vins
This shop offers an excellent selection of Hungarian and international wines; expert advice is also on hand.

✉ József Attila utca 12, Budapest V ☎ 317 5919 🕓 Mon–Fri 10–6, Sat 10–3

Hold utcai vásárcsarnok
Near Parliament, this food hall is a compact alternative to the massive Central Market for quality farm produce and much more.

✉ Hold utca 13, Budapest V ☎ 332 3976 🕓 Mon 6:30–5, Tue–Fri 6:30–6, Sat 6:30–2

Pick Salami Shop
Pick's flagship store in Budapest sells salami and other Pick products.

✉ Kossuth Lajos tér 9, Budapest V ☎ 331 7783; www.pick.hu
🕓 Mon–Fri 6–7

Szamos Marcipán
If you have a sweet tooth, you will love this store for its large and creative selection of marzipan delights.

✉ Párizsi utca 3, Budapest V ☎ 317 3643; www.szamosmarcipan.hu
🕓 Daily 10–7

GIFTS, JEWELLERY AND MUSIC
Folkart Centrum
Sells Hungarian-made folk art in the form of clothes, pottery, dolls and lacework at reasonable prices.

✉ Váci utca 58, Budapest V ☎ 318 5840; www.folkartcentrum.hu
🕓 Daily 10–7

Herend Porcelain
Here you can purchase a piece of world-famous Herend porcelain – although you may be put off by the price. There's another outlet on Andrássy út.

✉ József nádor tér 11, Budapest V ☎ 317 2622; www.herend.com
🕓 Mon–Fri 10–6, Sat 10–2

M. Frey Wille

Head here for colourful matching jewellery featuring Klimt and Egyptian motifs from the Vienna-based designers.

✉ Régiposta utca 19, Budapest V ☎ 318 7665; www.frey-wille.com

🕘 Mon–Fri 10–6, Sat 10–4

Porcelánház

As the name suggests, this folk shop specializes in porcelain and pottery, mainly from southeastern Hungary.

✉ Váci utca 45, Budapest V ☎ 266 3165; www.alfoldiporcelan.hu

🕘 Mon–Fri 10–6, Sat 10–3

Rózsavölgyi

This music shop (the largest in Central Europe) specializes in classical music and sheet music. Also folk and rock sections.

✉ Szervita tér 5, Budapest V ☎ 318 3500; www.lira.hu 🕘 Mon–Fri 10–6, Sat 10–2

ENTERTAINMENT

NIGHTLIFE

Beckett's

This great Irish-style pub serves good grub and beer and is frequented by homesick expats. It also screens rubgy matches.

✉ Bajcsy–Zsilinszky ut 72, Budapest V ☎ 311 1035; www.becketts.hu

🕘 Daily noon–1am

Fat Mo's

The weekend sees this elaborately furnished bar, with a prohibition-era theme, packed with visitors and executives. Its attractions are affordable Irish beers, decent bands and dancing.

✉ Nyári Pál utca 11, Budapest V ☎ 266 8027; www.fatmo.hu 🕘 Thu–Sat 5pm–3am, Sun–Wed 5pm–1am

Gödör Klub

Gödör Klub is one of the best concert venues in the centre.

✉ Erzsébet tér, Budapest V ☎ 06 20 201 3868; www.godorklub.hu

🕘 Fri–Sat 10pm–4am, Sun–Thu 10pm–2am

Living Room

A huge club with three rooms offering different music styles to dance to. The crowd is generally college age.

✉ Kossuth Lajos utca 17, Budapest V ☎ 06 30 992 9932; www.livingroom.hu 🕓 Wed–Sat 9pm–5am

Negro

The city's most renowned cocktail bar is close to Szent István Bazilika (► 50–51) and has outdoor seating.

✉ Szent István tér 11, Budapest V ☎ 302 0136; www.negrobar.hu
🕓 Mon–Tue 8pm–1am, Wed–Sun 8pm–2am

LIVE ARTS
Aranytíz Cultural Centre

A stalwart supporter of Hungarian folk culture, the Aranytíz focuses its attention on traditional music and dance. Its Saturday *Magyar táncház* (Hungarian dance house) is a riotous event.

✉ Arany János utca 10, Budapest V ☎ 354 3400; www.aranytiz.hu

Katona József Theatre

Katona József has arguably the highest theatre credentials in the country. It puts on both mainstream and alternative plays and its smaller venue, the Kamra, stages some equally fine performances.

✉ Petőfi Sándor utca 6, Budapest V ☎ 318 3725; www.katonajozsefszinhaz.hu

Merlin International Theatre

Close to the centre of Pest, the Merlin is a magical little theatre that hosts a plethora of plays in English.

✉ Gerlóczy utca 4, Budapest V ☎ 318 9338; www.merlinszinhaz.hu

Szent István Bazilika

Enjoy evening performances (usually beginning at 7) of classical, choral and orchestral music in this richly decorated and ornate church (► 50–51).

✉ Szent István tér 1, Budapest V ☎ 311 0839; www.basilica.hu

Terézváros, Erzsébetváros and Városliget

With some splendid entertainment venues and dozens of restaurants, cafes and bars, the buzz of modern Budapest is loudest in Terézváros (Teresa Town) and Erzsébetváros (Elisabeth Town). Városliget (City Park), further to the east, is an outdoor oasis in a very urban stretch of Budapest. It is a place where locals and visitors alike can relax, stroll, play and admire the few remaining tributes to the Magyar millennium celebrations of 1896.

Terézváros and Erzsébetváros also have their fair share of history, dating mainly from periods in the 19th and 20th centuries when the area profited from boom times and suffered terribly under the Nazis. Terézváros is the more northerly of the two districts. Secessionist treasures hide in its back streets, while

entertainment hot spots like the State Opera, Nagymező utca, Budapest's Broadway, and Liszt Ferenc tér are situated closer to the Danube. Most of Erzsébetváros' attractions are close to central Pest, known locally as the old Jewish quarter.

Terézváros

ANDRÁSSY ÚT (ANDRÁSSY AVENUE)

Once the city's premier boulevard, this World Heritage Site was named after the statesman Andrássy. An architectural jumble of glorious opulence and fading splendour, at one time it was known as Stalin Avenue, and until recently was called Avenue of the People's Republic. It runs all the way from City Park, and is home to the State Opera House and the Academy of Fine Arts – and an almost constant stream of traffic. The stretch up to Oktogon is lined with chic boutiques, while beyond that the boulevard widens to accommodate embassies and upmarket residential buildings.

➕ 5H–9P ✉ Andrássy út, Budapest V 🍴 Baraka (€€€, ➤ 152) 🚇 Oktogon

HOPP FERENC KELET-ÁZSIAI MÚVÉSZETI MÚZEUM (FERENC HOPP MUSEUM OF EASTERN ASIATIC ART)

This museum, one of two in the city devoted to major collections of Asian art, houses the treasures amassed by the Hungarian traveller Ferenc Hopp (1833–1919), who once lived here. It's a little gem, and tells you as much about Ferenc Hopp himself – a compulsive, eccentric collector – as about the treasures of East Asia. Among the fascinating ancient exhibits are Buddhist works and Indian art dating as far back as the third century. A collection of Chinese and Japanese exhibits are housed nearby in the Ráth György Múzeum at Városligeti fasor 12.
www.imm.hu

➕ 8Q ✉ Andrássy út 103, Budapest V ☎ 322 8476 🕐 Tue–Sun 10–6
💰 Moderate 🍴 Lukács (€€, ➤ 155) 🚇 M1 Bajza utca 🚌 Bus: 105

LISZT FERENC EMLÉKMÚZEUM (FERENC LISZT MEMORIAL MUSEUM)

In 1986, three rooms of the apartment where Liszt spent the last six years of his life were turned into a museum celebrating his musical genius. His musical library, original sheet music and black-

and-white photos make good browsing for Liszt fans. The few highlights scattered throughout include Liszt's "composing desk", sporting a three-octave keyboard, a piano with glass slices instead of strings and Liszt's warts-and-all death mask.

www.lisztmuseum.hu

➕ 8R ✉ Vörösmarty utca 35, Budapest VI ☎ 322 9804 ⏰ Mon–Fri 10–6, Sat 9–5 ✋ Inexpensive 🍴 Lukács (€€, ➤ 155) Ⓜ M1 Vörösmarty utca

MAGYAR ÁLLAMI OPERAHÁZ (STATE OPERA HOUSE)

Best places to see, ➤ 42–43.

NYUGATI PÁLYAUDVAR
(WESTERN RAILWAY STATION)

Since trains depart from here for the north and east, the name is perhaps slightly misleading – it's named after the train company. Constructed in the late 19th century by the Eiffel company (responsible for the famous Parisian tower), over the following hundred years the hall deteriorated and plans were drawn up for a new building. Conservationists protested and won the day, helping

to preserve the principal iron structure. Towards the end of the hall on the left is a large door, above which is carved the old Austro-Hungarian motto: *Viribus Units* (With Unity Strength). Beyond the door is the opulent Royal Lounge. The elegant glass screen of the station's main facade lets the trains merge with the city's traffic. The giant restaurant to the right of the main entrance is now a McDonald's, though they have retained the elegance of the room.

➕ 5F ✉ Teréz körút 55–57, Budapest VI ☎ 349 0115 ⏱ Open access
🍴 Dzsungel (€€, ➤ 152) 🚇 Nyugati pályaudvar 🚊 Tram: 4, 6

POSTAMÚZEUM (POSTAL MUSEUM)

The Postal Museum was formerly a luxurious seven-room private apartment in the once affluent area of Sugárút. The owner's initials "AS" (Andreás Saxlehner) can be seen all over the house. Most sumptuous of all are the Károly Lotz frescoes on the staircase. Apart from the portable furniture, most of the fittings and furniture are original. Attendants will put into operation some of the exhibits. You can even see a section of a pneumatic exchange.

www.postamuzeum.hu

➕ 5H ✉ Andrássy út 3, Budapest VI ☎ 269 6838 ⏱ Tue–Sun 10–6
✋ Inexpensive 🍴 Goa (€€), Andrássy út 8; daily 12–12 🚇 M1 Bajcsy-Zsilinszky út, M1/2/3 Deák tér 🚌 Bus: 105

TERROR HÁZA (HOUSE OF TERROR)

The hideous Russian tank crouched toadlike at the foot of the light well of this grim courtyard building sets the tone for the horrifying tales recounted inside. Once the headquarters of the Arrow Cross, the home-grown Hungarian Nazis, after 1945 the edifice passed into the ownership of the communist secret police.

Since 2002 it has housed sophisticated displays (with full commentaries in English) that expertly evoke some of the darker sides of Hungary's recent past: arbitrary rule, deportation, genocide, forced resettlement, torture and murder. A visit to the House of Terror is a sobering experience and an essential

introduction to the country's tormented history in the 20th century, despite claims that the displays put excessive emphasis on communist crimes and not enough on the atrocities of the Arrow Cross and Hungarian anti-Semitism.

➕ 7R ✉ Andrássy út 60 ☎ 374 2600 🕐 Tue–Sun 10–6 ✋ Expensive 🍴 Lukács (€€, ➤ 155) Ⓜ M1 Vörösmarty utca 🚌 Bus: 105

ZENEAKADÉMIA (ACADEMY OF MUSIC)

The Academy of Music, another of Miksa Róth's impressive art nouveau gems, was completed in 1907. The Academy was founded in 1875 (in a different building). Its first president was the great Hungarian composer Franz Liszt (a bronze statue of him stands above the main entrance), and its first director was Ferenc Erkel, the father of Hungarian grand opera. The main hall seats 1,200, and is dominated by the magnificent Walcker organ. On each side of the organ there are inscriptions in Latin: *Sursum Corda* (Raise Your Hearts) on the left; and *Favete Linguis* (Shut Up, or Be Quiet) on the right. A beautiful building, the Academy is the centre of Budapest's musical life.

www.zeneakademia.hu

➕ 7S ✉ Liszt Ferenc tér 8, Budapest VI ☎ 462 4600 🕐 From 10am to performance end ✋ Ticket prices vary 🍴 Menza (€€, ➤ 154) Ⓜ M1 Oktogon 🚃 Tram: 4, 6

Erzsébetváros

NAGY ZSINAGÓGA (GREAT SYNAGOGUE)

At the intersection of Dohány utca and Károly körút, at the heart of the old Jewish quarter, stands the Great Synagogue, the largest in Europe. Above the entrance the Hebrew line reads: "Make me a sanctuary and I will dwell among them". With its three naves and flat ceiling, the building holds just under 3,000 worshippers: 1,492 men on the ground floor and 1,472 women in the gallery. One of the buildings in the compound was the birthplace of Theodor Herzl, father of the Zionist movement. Built in Moorish-Byzantine style, the synagogue has two magnificent domes rising to 43m (141ft).

The Holocaust Memorial in the back garden is directly over the mass graves dug during the 1944–45 Hungarian Fascist period, and on every leaf is the name of a martyr. The memorial is a grim reminder of the suffering of the Hungarian Jews, and of their determination never to forget. The walls of some buildings near the synagogue still bear bullet marks.

www.dohany-zsinagoga.hu

✚ 6J ✉ Dohány utca 2–8, Budapest VII ☎ 462 0477 🕐 Mid-Apr to Oct Sun–Thu 10–5, Fri 10–2; Nov to mid-Apr Sun–Thu 10–3, Fri 10–2 🖐 Expensive 🍴 Spinoza (€€–€€€, ➤ 154) 🚇 M2 Astoria 🚌 Bus: 7. Tram: 47, 49. Trolleybus: 74

NEW YORK KÁVÉHÁZ (NEW YORK CAFÉ)

To some the New York Café is the pinnacle of Budapest's cafe culture, to others it's an exaggerated eyesore; either way, there is no denying its history. Now part of a five-star hotel, the New York began life in 1894 as part of the New York Palace. From its very beginning, it was *the* literary cafe, attracting the city's top writers and artists in droves. For decades it remained open day and night year-round, until the aftermath of war and the 1930s depression forced its closure in 1947.

It remained closed until the 21st century and opened its doors in 2006 after a complete refurbishment in Italian neo-Renaissance style. The cafe today lacks any warmth or cosiness – traits of a top coffeehouse – but it does have grandeur: a row of winged Pan statues adorns the facade, and the interior is embellished with plush red seating, frescoed ceilings, twisted gold columns, giant mirrors and an army of chandeliers. The attached hotel is also worth a peek (➤ 151).

www.newyorkcafe.hu

➕ 8T ✉ Erzsébet körút 9–11, Budapest VII ☎ 886 6111 🕐 Daily 10am–midnight 🎟 Free 🚇 M2 Blaha Lujza tér

RÓTH MIKSA EMLÉKHÁZ (MIKSA RÓTH MEMORIAL HOUSE)

See works by the art nouveau artist Miksa Róth (1865–1944) at his former residence on Nefelejcs utca. Róth, who lived and worked here from 1911 until his death, is best known for his stunning stained-glass pieces, but he also created gorgeous mosaics, which are displayed at the house. The surprisingly bland living quarters are still filled with Róth's original furniture. Further examples of his genius are found around the city, at the Gresham Palace (➤ 122), the Országház (➤ 48–49) and the Zeneakadémia (➤ 141).

www.rothmuzeum.hu

➕ 9S ✉ Nefelejcs utca 26, Budapest VII ☎ 341 6789 🕐 Tue–Sun 2pm–6pm 🎟 Inexpensive 🚇 M2 Keleti pályaudvar 🚌 Trolleybus: 73, 74, 76

a walk around the VI District

The most illustrious part of the city in the late 19th century, the VI District is now a mixture of dilapidation and residual glamour.

Start at the State Opera House on Andrássy út.

Though often congested with traffic now, Andrássy út was once the Champs-Élysées of Budapest, and its neo-Renaissance and baroque opera house (► 42) is one of the finest in Europe.

Walk up towards Oktogon and look out for the magnificent Művész Coffee House and the Párizsi Áruház at No 29.

The latter was once an exclusive casino, and some of its former glory remains. It has been recently restored and now houses a bookshop and offices.

Past the grand villas is the Lukács Coffee House (▶ 155), newly restored to its former splendour, and the Kodály körönd, sumptuously painted with delicate gold filigree. After the Kodály körönd, go right along Bajza utca, past the old villas and diplomatic residences, to Városligeti fasor.

In the 19th century, this grand boulevard with tree-lined pavements (sidewalks) was used for horse racing. Here at the boundary of the VI District you will see some wonderful art nouveau villas and mansions.

Take a quiet break in the Epreskert, or Mulberry Garden, half-way along Bajza utca.

This is the Arts Academy sculpture garden, with both baroque sculptures and modern works.

Meander back via Király utca and Hunyadi tér to the heart of the district. At the intersection with Erzsébet körút, turn right and head towards Liszt Ferenc tér on the left side.

Here is the Academy of Music (▶ 141).

Turn left onto Andrássy út and return to the State Opera House.

Distance 4–5km (2.5–3 miles)
Time 2–3 hours, or 5 hours with stops for refreshments and visits
Start/end point State Opera House ✚ 5G 🚇 M1 Opera
Lunch Lukács (€, ▶ 155)

Városliget

VÁROSLIGET
(CITY PARK)

City Park is the biggest of its kind in Budapest, and you can find just about every form of entertainment for children, as well as tranquillity for adults. Standing on an island in the boating lake is the fairy-tale Vajdahunyad vár (castle). Nearby, the beautiful art nouveau Állatkert (Zoo, ► 62) is a perennial favourite with children,

especially the "Animal Kindergarten," where newborn animals are kept. Next to the Zoo is the Fővárosi Nagycirkusz (Municipal Circus, ➤ 62). The Vidámpark (Amusement Park, ➤ 63) is also very popular, with a carousel, roller coaster, Ferris wheel, enchanted castle and slot-machine hall.

The lavish **Széchenyi Gyógyfürdő** (thermal baths, ➤ 67) are the largest of their kind in Europe. Here you'll find the locals playing chess while relaxing in the thermal pools. There are various indoor and outdoor areas, but the outdoor baths, with their whirlpools and shoulder-pounding fountains, should not be missed.

Towards the southwest corner of the City Park you'll find the Közlekedési Múzeum (Transport Museum, ➤ 149) and nearby the charming Garden for the Blind. Of interest also is Petőfi Csarnok (Petőfi Hall), a bastion of rock and pop music. It also plays host to a flea market on weekends, a theatre for children, a roller-skating club and a Saturday-evening disco.

✚ Vajdahunyad vár 10P; Állatkert 9N; Fővárosi Nagycirkusz 9N–10N; Vidámpark 10N; Közlekedési Múzeum 11P; Petőfi Csarnok 10P

Széchenyi Gyógyfürdő

✚ 10N ✉ Állatkerti körút 11, Budapest XIV ☎ 363 3210 ⏰ Daily 6am–10pm ✋ Expensive 🚇 M1 Széchenyi Fürdő 🚍 Trolleybus: 72

GUNDEL ÉTTEREM (GUNDEL RESTAURANT)

It's not unusual in Budapest to come across restaurants and cafes that are worth visiting not just for their food but also for their architecture and decor. The unique thing about Gundel is its first-rate collection of Hungarian masters on the walls; the menu helpfully supplies information about the paintings. Above the splendid dining room are the Elisabeth and Andrássy rooms, where some of the city's most elegant banquets are held. The food is excellent and there's a seriously well-stocked wine cellar.

www.gundel.hu

✚ 9P ✉ Állatkerti körút 2, Budapest XIV ☎ 889 8100 ⏰ Daily 12–4, 6:30–12 (Sun brunch 11:30–3) 🚇 M1 Hősök tere

HŐSÖK TERE (HEROES' SQUARE)

Heroes' Square sits at the top of Andrássy út, where it meets City
Park. The square forms a splendid unity of two architecturally
diverse buildings – the Art Gallery and the Museum of Fine Arts –
and a monument. The central feature of Heroes' Square is the
Millennium Monument, a 36m (118ft) column, on top of which
stands Gabriel, the Guardian Angel. The colonnades on either side

display statues of Hungarian kings and leading figures of the Hungarian independence wars. On the left wing are the allegorical bronze statues of War, Peace and Knowledge; on the right, statues representing War, Peace and Glory. In the middle of the square, behind the column of Gabriel, is the picturesque group of statues of the conquering Magyars, with Árpád, the leading reigning prince, in the middle. The statue complex commemorates the 1,000th year of the Hungarian state. Dedicated to the nation's heroes, its architectural design is particularly fitting, and leaves you with a deep sense of Hungarians' pride in their past.

Next to Heroes' Square is Procession Square, where processions and parades are held on public holidays. This was the site of a monolithic statue of Stalin that was torn down by Hungarian nationalists during the 1956 Uprising. Also here is the Tomb of the Unknown Soldier, where Soviet veterans still come to pay their respects.

🚩 9P 🖂 Budapest XIV 🕓 Open access 🍴 Robinson (€€–€€€, ➤ 59)
🚇 M1 Hősök tere 🚌 Bus: 20E, 30, 105. Trolleybus: 70, 74, 75, 79

KÖZLEKEDÉSI MÚZEUM (TRANSPORT MUSEUM)

The exhibits here include beautifully accurate models as well as examples of the real thing: ships, cars, motorbikes and locomotives and rolling stock. A spacious hall 200m (220yds) from the main building houses aeroplanes and fascinating aviation memorabilia. The museum has a number of outstations, including a display of commercial aircraft at Ferihegy airport (➤ 26).
www.km.iif.hu

🚩 11P 🖂 Városligeti körút 11, Budapest XIV ☎ 273 3840 🕓 Apr–Oct Tue–Fri 10–5, Sat–Sun 10–6; Nov–Mar Tue–Fri 10–4, Sat–Sun 10–5
💰 Moderate 🍴 Small bar (€) in a converted railway carriage next to the museum (daily 12–12) 🚌 Bus: 7, 173. Tram: 1. Trolleybus: 70, 72, 74

SZÉPMŰVÉSZETI MÚZEUM (FINE ARTS MUSEUM)

Best places to see, ➤ 52–53.

HOTELS

Andrássy Hotel (€€€)
Just off the prestigous Andrássy út, this tasteful, luxurious hotel was once the exclusive guest house of the Foreign Ministry.
✉ Andrássy út 111, Budapest VI ☎ 462 2100; www.andrassyhotel.com

Corinthia Grand Hotel (€€€)
Originally built at the time of the millennium celebrations in 1896, this city institution on the Outer Ring has been fully restored to its former glory. It's a tasteful combination of tradition and modernity.
✉ Erzsébet körút 43–49, Budapest VII ☎ 479 4000; www.corinthiahotels.com

Domina Fiesta (€€)
Clean lines and plenty of colour dominate the rooms in this hotel, at the top end of Király utca, as close as you can get to the major sights, entertainment hubs and shopping districts.
✉ Király utca 20, Budapest VI ☎ 328 3000; www.dominahotels.com

Hotel Pest (€€)
An 18th-century town house in suburban Pest with simple, modern rooms. Within strolling distance of the Magyar Állami Operaház (▶ 42), bar-clad Liszt Ferenc tér and the highlights of Belváros.
✉ Paulay Ede utca 31, Budapest VI ☎ 343 1198; www.hotelpest.hu

K + K Hotel Opera (€€)
This hotel was specially built for music lovers and is just 50m (55yds) from the Opera House. Guests are treated to immaculate service and can make use of the leisure facilities.
✉ Révay útca 24, Budapest VI ☎ 269 0222; www.kkhotels.com

Mamaison Residence Izabella (€€€)
These spacious apartments have wooden floors and modern amenities. Many face the quiet courtyard and offer private balconies.
✉ Izabella utca 61, Budapest VI ☎ 475 5900; www.residenceizabella.com

Medosz (€)

Basic accommodation, still breathing the atmosphere of the not-so-good old days pre-1989, when it provided lodgings for provincial trade unionists and the party faithful summoned to the metropolis. It's in a great location, however, near the Opera and the nightlife on Liszt Ferenc tér.

✉ Jókai tér 9, Budapest VI ☎ 374 3001; www.medoszhotel.hu

New York Palace (€€€)

This luxury establishment sports immaculate rooms filled with delicate antiques, fine art and the latest hotel technology. Attached is the New York Kávéház (➤ 143).

✉ Erzsébet körút 9–11, Budapest VII ☎ 886 6111; www.boscolohotels.com

Radisson Blu Béke (€€)

A large, modernized hotel on the city's main thoroughfare, the Grand Boulevard. Good eating can be had in Olive's Restaurant and the elegant Zsolnay Café serves sweets and espresso.

✉ Teréz körút 43, Budapest VI ☎ 889 3900; www.radissonblu.com

Regency Suites Budapest (€€€)

These spacious, modern apartments are opposite Deák Ferenc tér, making this an ideal location for business visitors. The hotel also boasts a conference room and a roof terrace – perfect for relaxing after a long day.

✉ Madách Imre tér 2, Budapest VII ☎ 801 6300; www.regencysuites.hu

RESTAURANTS

Abszint (€€)

See page 58.

Bagolyvár (€€)

Attached to Gundel restaurant (➤ 58), the "Owl Castle" provides "home-style" Hungarian food served in a convivial atmosphere (and at cheaper prices than Gundel).

✉ Állatkerti út 2, Budapest VI ☎ 468 3110; www.bagolyvar.com
🕔 Daily 12–11

Baraka (€€€)

Baraka has a wildly inviting seasonal menu including pan-seared monkfish, wild duck breast, and salmon in wasabi crust.

✉ Andrássy Hotel, Andrássy út 111, Budapest VI ☎ 483 1355; www.barakarestaurant.hu 🕐 Daily 12–3, 6–11

Belcanto (€€)

This restaurant is by the State Opera House and its waiters sing songs from well-known operas. Good international cuisine.

✉ Dalszinház utca 8, Budapest VI ☎ 269 2786; www.belcanto.hu 🕐 Daily 12–3, 4:30pm–2am

Bouchon (€€–€€€)

Bouchon's modern international menu includes steamed pike-perch with vegetables and rosemary-saffron potatoes, and roasted veal "Shaslik" with garlic and spicy mixed salad.

✉ Zichy Jenő utca 33, Budapest VI ☎ 353 4094; www.cafebouchon.hu 🕐 Mon–Sat 9am–11pm

Chez Daniel (€€)

A small, select menu of excellent French dishes is carefully prepared. Good wine and beer list. Book ahead.

✉ Szív utca 32, Budapest VI ☎ 302 4039; www.chezdaniel.hu 🕐 Daily 12–3, 7–11

Dzsungel (€€)

A restaurant dedicated to all things "jungly", where the menu dazzles with exotically named dishes and there's foliage all around.

✉ Jókai utca 30, Budapest VI ☎ 302 4003; www.dzsungelcafe.hu 🕐 Daily noon–1am

Fausto's (€€€)

Ranks among the best restaurants in the city, and serves creative Italian dishes in stylish surroundings. Osteria is its less formal sister restaurant, on Dohány utca.

✉ Szekely Mihály utca 2, Budapest VI ☎ 877 6210; www.fausto.hu 🕐 Mon–Fri 12–3, 7–11, Sat 6–11

Gundel (€€€)

See pages 58 and 147.

Hanna (€€)

Immerse yourself further in the ambience of the Jewish Quarter by having a tasty kosher lunch in the light and airy dining hall attached to the Orthodox synagogue.

✉ Dob utca 35, Budapest VII ☎ 342 1072; www.koserhanna.hu 🕐 Daily 8am–10pm. Closed Sat evening

Indigo (€€)

Budapest is not overly endowed with Indian restaurants, and that makes this classy restaurant a rare find. The food, cooked by northern Indian chefs, is excellent.

✉ Jókai utca 13, Budapest VI ☎ 428 2187; www.indigo-restaurant.hu 🕐 Daily 12–11

Kispipa (€€€)

Stiff but attentive service, old-fashioned Hungarian and international cuisine and live piano music (from 7pm).

✉ Akácfa utca 38, Budapest VII ☎ 342 2587; www.kispipa.hu 🕐 Daily noon–1am

Klassz (€)

The food here is excellent yet modestly priced. It's a member of the Bortársaság (Wine Society, ➤ 102) and you can purchase their wines on the spot. The no-reservation policy means that it can be difficult to get a table at peak hours.

✉ Andrássy út 41, Budapest VI ☎ 328 0081 🕐 Mon–Sat 11:30–11, Sun 11:30–6

Marquis de Salade (€€)

A unique animal in Budapest, Marquis de Salade specializes in Azerbaijani food. There are Russian and Hungarian dishes thrown into the mix, and a few vegetarian options.

✉ Hajós utca 43, Budapest VI ☎ 302 4086; www.marquisdesalade.hu 🕐 Daily noon–1am

Menza (€€)

The consciously retro regime of 1960s floral wallpaper, plastic booths and Formica finish is a refreshing change from Liszt Ferenc tér's swathe of modern establishments. Young socialites and business-lunchers flock here for Hungarian standards with a modern twist.

✉ Liszt Ferenc tér 2, Budapest VI ☎ 413 1482; www.menzaetterem.hu
🕒 Daily 10am–midnight

Napos Oldal (€)

This vegetarian cafe and health shop is named after the side of the street on which it sits (sunny side) and offers fresh salads and pastries. Staff are super-friendly.

✉ Jókai utca 7, Budapest VI ☎ 354 0048; www.naposoldal.com 🕒 Mon–Fri 10–8, Sat 10–2

Robinson (€€–€€€)

See page 59.

Spinoza (€€–€€€)

This polished eatery in the heart of the Jewish District serves Hungarian and Jewish dishes (including breakfast) in relaxed surroundings. There's also theatre and live music some nights.

✉ Dob utca 15, Budapest VII ☎ 413 7488; www.spinozahaz.hu 🕒 Daily 8am–11pm

CAFES

Bobek

Named after a rabbit in a Czech cartoon, Bobek is a colourful, laid-back cafe. Light bites are available alongside the extensive drinks menu and there's a heated garden area in winter.

✉ Kazinczy utca 53, Budapest VII ☎ 322 0729; www.bobek.hu 🕒 Mon–Thu 10am–midnight, Fri 10am–2am, Sat 11am–2am, Sun 11–11

Café Vian

Vian has a lively buzz and excellent desserts. Floor-to-ceiling windows in winter and pavement seating in summer allow unabridged views of Liszt Ferenc tér. Pick up a coffee or cocktail and watch the comings and goings.

✉ Liszt Ferenc tér 9, Budapest VI ☎ 268 1154; www.cafevian.com 🕐 Daily 9am–1am ❓ There can be a wait when things get busy

Lukács

Almost everything about Lukács is refined, from its divine selection of cakes to its elegant turn-of-the-20th-century interior.

✉ Andrássy út 70, Budapest VI ☎ 373 0407; www.lukacscukraszda.com 🕐 Mon–Fri 8:30–7, Sat 9–7, Sun 9:30–7

Művész

Művész ("artist") is a century-old cafe with classical trimmings, and one of the best spots to sit and watch the world go by.

✉ Andrássy út 29, Budapest VI ☎ 343 3544; www.muveszkavehaz.hu 🕐 Mon–Sat 9am–10pm, Sun 10–10

New York Kávéház (New York Café)

This splendid and famous old establishment (► 143) was restored to its former state and reopened as part of a luxury hotel.

✉ Erzsébet körút 9–11, Budapest VII ☎ 886 6111; www.newyorkcafe.hu 🕐 Daily 7am–10pm

Szamos Marzipan Café

A luxurious combination of the Szamos Marzipan Café on the premises of the elegant Corinthia Grand Hotel (► 150). The cakes are excellent, and the children will love the tiny marzipan figurines.

✉ Erzsébet körút 43–49, Budapest VII ☎ 413 7968; www.corinthia.com 🕐 Daily 10–8

SHOPPING

Haas & Czjek

This shop sells famous Hungarian porcelain brands like Herend and Zsolnay, as well as international names such as Swarovski and Wedgwood.

✉ Bajcsy-Zsilinszky út 23, Budapest VI ☎ 311 4094; www.porcelan.hu 🕐 Mon–Fri 10–7, Sat 10–3

Liszt Ferenc Music Shop

A music-lover's paradise, a few hundred yards from the Opera House. Here you will find works by Hungarian artists, including sheets of folk music by Kodály and Bartók, and translations of Hungarian novels.

✉ Andrássy út 45, Budapest VI ☎ 352 7314; www.lisztbolt.hu 🕐 Mon–Fri 10–7, Sat 10–1

Tisza Cipő

The communist-era sportswear sold here is all the go in Budapest.

✉ Károly körút 1, Budapest VII ☎ 266 3055; www.tiszacipo.hu 🕐 Mon–Fri 10–7, Sat 10–1

ENTERTAINMENT

NIGHTLIFE

Café Eklektika

While it has a mixed clientele, this cafe-bar just off Andrássy út is run by a lesbian couple and is gay-friendly. There are live jazz performances and female-only nights every month.

✉ Nagymező utca 30, Budapest VI ☎ 266 1226; www.eklektika.hu
🕐 Daily 12–12

Castro Bisztro

A small, smoky, atmospheric pub under the arcades of Madách tér, this Serbian bistro is a hidden gem, favoured by locals and tourists alike. The drinks are inexpensive.

✉ Madách tér 3, Budapest VII ☎ 215 0184 🕐 Mon–Thu 9am–midnight, Fri 9am–1am, Sat 2pm–1am, Sun 2pm–midnight

Fészek Club

An occasionally crazy club with a lively vibe and plenty of late-night drinkers. The cellar bar has cushioned booths and a small stage.

✉ Kertész utca 36, Budapest VII ☎ 342 6549; www.feszek-muveszklub.hu
🕐 8pm–6am

Instant

Instant came to life a few years ago, and quicky became one of the trendiest places in town. The club is in a block of derelict flats.

✉ Nagymező utca 38, Budapest VI ☎ 311 0704; www.instant.co.hu

🕐 Daily 4pm–5am

Karma

An Asian-themed bar that gets rave reviews from locals, serving
Hungarian and Asian dishes. Situated on Liszt Ferenc tér, it is the
perfect place for people-watching.

✉ Liszt Ferenc tér 11, Budapest VI ☎ 413 6764; www.karmabudapest.com

🕐 Daily 11am–2am

Morrison's Music Pub

A popular club next to the Opera House, Morrison's is a firm
favourite with Budapesters and expats, as well as tourists. The
music is a mix of cheesy retro and modern. Another branch near
Nyugati targets students, offering cheap beer from 5pm.

✉ Révay utca 25, Budapest VI ☎ 269 4060 🕐 Mon–Fri 7pm–4am

Moulin Rouge

Low lights, red velvet and golden chandeliers dominate this club,
where DJs play a range of favourite tunes. The upstairs bar area is
dominated by a king-sized bed!

✉ Nagymező utca 17, Budapest VI ☎ 06 30 434 9995 🕐 Wed, Fri–Sat 9–5

Old Man's Music Pub

Designed like a faded living room, the Old Man's Pub features blues
and soul performances nightly (followed by a DJ until the early
hours), with good pizzas and other dishes on the menu.

✉ Akácfa utca13, Budapest VII ☎ 322 7645; www.oldmansmusicpub.com

🕐 Daily 3pm–4am

Pótkulcs

Although hidden behind a nondescript fence, the "Spare Key"
is a welcoming bar that's filled with sagging furniture and a
relaxed crowd.

✉ Csengery utca 65/b, Budapest VI ☎ 269 1050; www.potkulcs.hu

🕐 Sun–Tue 5pm–1:30am, Thu–Sat 5pm–2:30am

Szimpla and Szimpla Kert

Szimpla is a lovely bohemian bar, with worn wooden floors and a rabble of mismatching furniture, covering three levels. Szimpla Kert is an outdoor sister bar a short distance away.

✉ Kertész utca 48, Budapest VII ☎ 321 9119; www.szimpla.hu
🕙 Daily 10am–2am

LIVE ARTS

Central Europe Dance Theatre

Folk and contemporary dance performances representing regional culture are staged here.

✉ Bethlen Gábor tér 3, Budapest VII ☎ 342 7163; www.ket.szinhaz.org
🕙 Closed in summer

Magyar Állami Operaház (State Opera House)

World opera at one of the finest and most beautiful opera houses in Europe. Suitable for the aficionado and amateur alike (► 42–43).

✉ Andrássy út 22, Budapest VI ☎ 353 0170; www.opera.hu

Nádor Concert Hall

Inside the Institute of the Blind, on the corner of City Park, this concert hall – built in secessionist style – hosts concerts every weekend (October–May). Tickets are available on the spot.

✉ Ajtósi-Dürer sor 39, Budapest XIV ☎ 363 3343; www.vakisk.hu

Operettszínház (Operetta Theatre)

The unrivalled venue for the best of Hungarian operetta and not to be missed.

✉ Nagymező utca 19, Budapest VI ☎ 312 4866; www.operettszinhaz.hu

Petőfi Csarnok

Petőfi Csarnok hosts medium-sized rock concerts in Városliget. There's a flea market here every Saturday.

✉ Zichy Mihály út 14, Budapest XIV ☎ 363 3730; www.petoficsarnok.hu

Zeneakadémia (Academy of Music)

See page 141.

Józsefváros and Ferencváros

Józsefváros (Joseph Town) and Ferencváros (Francis Town) have the same general make-up – solidly working class with a large dose of grit. Many buildings, particularly west of Pest's big ring road Nagykörút, are in a run-down state, but among the dilapidated dwellings are a handful of superb museums and state-of-the-art concert and theatre halls.

To the north, Józsefváros is largely bereft of sights aside from the excellent Magyar Nemzeti Múzeum (Hungarian National Museum, ➤ 160–161) and peaceful Kerepesi temető (Kerepes Cemetery, ➤ 160).

Ferencváros is almost double the size of Józsefváros but much

of its southern extreme is of little interest, criss-crossed by rail tracks and dotted with industrial sites. Inside the Nagykörút is another matter; this urban playground is home to the Vásárcsarnok (Central Market Hall, ➤ 165), the Iparművészeti Múzeum (Museum of Applied Arts, ➤ 162) and restaurant-studded Ráday utca. Two of the city's newest cultural venues, the Művészetek Palotája (Palace of Arts, ➤ 164–165) and Nemzeti Színház (National Theatre, ➤ 165) are also here.

Józsefváros

KEREPESI TEMETŐ (KEREPES CEMETERY)

Kerepes is the official burial place of Hungary's national heroes. The largest mausoleums belong to Lajos Batthyány, Ferenc Deák and Lajos Kossuth. Batthyány, the first prime minister of Hungary, is honoured by a wide set of stairs guarded by lions, while Kossuth, a seminal leader in the 1848–49 War of Independence, is entombed in an enormous stone pagoda structure. The most central of the three, to Deák, an important statesman during the Dual Monarchy, is a domed affair topped by a wreath-bearing angel. Other noteworthy figures buried in the cemetery include the poets Endre Ady and Attila József, architects Ödön Lechner and Alajos Stróbl, and actress Lujza Blaha. Near the gate is the massive Pantheon to the Working Class Movement, used as a burial ground for the country's socialist leaders; the inscription above the mausoleum reads "They lived for communism and the people".

✚ 11U ✉ Fiumei út 16, Budapest VIII ☎ 333 9125 🕔 May–Jul daily 7am–8pm; Apr, Aug 7–7; Sep 7–6; Mar, Oct 7–5; Nov–Feb 7:30–5
✋ Free 🚇 Keleti 🚌 Bus: 7, 173. Tram: 24, 28, 62

MAGYAR NEMZETI MÚZEUM (HUNGARIAN NATIONAL MUSEUM)

The dignified neoclassical building set back in its own gardens is a dominant feature on the city's inner ring boulevard, Múzeum körút. It was completed in 1847, just in time for the ardent rebels of 1848 to use its broad steps as a platform for proclaiming their revolution with a spirited rendering of the *National Song*, composed for the occasion by the young poet Sándor Petőfi.

Inside are a central rotunda, a dome and a magnificent double staircase with wall-paintings.

A treasure-house of every kind of artefact, the museum gives a comprehensive and fascinating account of the course of Hungarian history and prehistory.

A section entitled "On the East–West Frontier" traces the evolution of the inhabitants of the Carpathian Basin from 400,000BC to AD804. A variety of up-to-the-minute techniques enlivens the story. You can see the reconstruction of a 6,000-year-old house, walk over prehistoric skeletons in their graves and confront a Bronze-Age warrior with sword and helmet.

The rich and extensive displays illustrating Hungarian history since the conversion to Christianity of King Stephen in 1000 are more static, but no less intriguing.

www.mnm.hu

➕ 6K ✉ Múzeum körút 14–16, Budapest VIII ☎ 338 2122 🕐 Tue–Sun 10–6 👤 Moderate Ⓜ M2 Astoria, M3 Kálvin tér 🚌 Bus: 9. Tram: 47, 49

MAGYAR TERMÉSZETTUDOMÁNYI MÚZEUM (HUNGARIAN NATURAL HISTORY MUSEUM)

A fun excursion for those with kids in tow. A huge whale gliding above the foyer is a sign of things to come. To the right once you enter the museum proper is an underwater hall with fresh- and saltwater aquariums and a coral-reef display under glass flooring. The older section of the museum covers three floors. The first floor has a menagerie of stuffed animals and minerals from the Carpathian Basin. A small Ark, with endangered species neatly packed inside, occupies one end of the second floor, where much of the remaining space deals with man's impact on the environment. The museum also makes a good stab at detailing early human existence in Hungary.

www.nhmus.hu

➕ 10W ✉ Ludovika tér 2–6, Budapest VIII ☎ 210 1085 🕐 Wed–Mon 10–6 🍴 Cafe (€) 👤 Permanent exhibitions: inexpensive; temporary exhibitions: moderate Ⓜ M3 Klinikák

Ferencváros

HOLOKAUSZT EMLÉKKÖZPONT
(HOLOCAUST MUSEUM)

On the site of a synagogue all but destroyed in World War II, this centre is an exhibition space and education facility funded by the government. The modern structure is split into three parts: a reconstructed synagogue where temporary exhibitions are held; a new wing containing the permanent "From Deprivation of Rights to Genocide"; and a Memorial Wall engraved with the names of Holocaust victims. The permanent exhibition spotlights the plight of Jews, Roma and other persecuted persons during the Nazi regime, but primarily focuses on three families. Photos, videos and private effects line the walls, providing a very personal account of the Holocaust. Each room deals with the ever-increasing phases of persecution; from the deprivation of rights, to the loss of property, freedom, human dignity and finally life.

www.hdke.hu

✚ 8W ✉ Páva utca 39, Budapest IX ☎ 455 3333 🕔 Tue–Sun 10–6 ✋ Moderate 🍴 Pink Cadillac (€€, ➤ 167) Ⓜ M3 Ferenc körút 🚋 Tram: 4, 6

IPARMŰVÉSZETI MÚZEUM
(MUSEUM OF APPLIED ARTS)

This fine museum was restored in the 1950s after it was badly damaged during World War II. The original building was one of hundreds built to mark the millennial celebrations of 1896. The coloured ceramic-and-brick building blends an art nouveau style with Hungarian folk motifs, which makes it a museum piece in itself. The main hall is covered with a steel-framed glass ceiling. The museum has fine collections of furniture, metalwork, textiles, woodwork, ceramics and glass, as well as other handicrafts.

www.imm.hu

✚ 8W ✉ Üllői út 33–7, Budapest IX ☎ 456 5100 🍴 Costes (€€€, ➤ 166) 🕔 Tue–Sun 10–6 ✋ Expensive Ⓜ M3 Ferenc körút 🚋 Tram: 4, 6

MŰVÉSZETEK PALOTÁJA (PALACE OF ARTS) AND LUDWIG MÚZEUM BUDAPEST

The Palace of Arts, which incorporates the Ludwig Museum Budapest, is the city's latest cultural offering. For some it's also the greatest, for it is home to the National Philharmonic and contemporary art in Budapest; it also shares a lonely stretch of the Pest embankment with the Nemzeti Színház (National Theatre, ► 165). Architecturally, it is quite bland, but its performance halls are exceptional, employing the latest technology to create the finest acoustics in the city.

The Ludwig covers three floors in the Palace's western wing with the city's premier collection of contemporary art. Hungarian

artists feature strongly, but it's the big international names that steal the show; look for Andy Warhol's *Single Elvis* (1964), Pablo Picasso's *Musketeer with Sword* (1972), Roy Lichtenstein's *Vicki* (1964) and Chuck Close's *Nat* (1972–73). The museum's calendar features temporary exhibitions of current artists from Hungary and abroad, although it mainly focuses on the work of Central and Eastern European artists.

🚇 8Z ✉ Komor Marcell utca 1, Budapest IX 🍴 Café (€) 🚋 Tram: 1, 2, 24

Művészetek Palotája

☎ 555 3000; www.mupa.hu 🕓 Daily 10–10. Ticket office: Mon–Fri 1–6, Sat–Sun 10–6

Ludwig Múzeum Budapest

☎ 555 3444; www.ludwigmuseum.hu 🕓 Tue–Sun 10–8
✋ Permanent exhibitions: inexpensive; temporary exhibitions: expensive

NEMZETI SZÍNHÁZ (NATIONAL THEATRE)

www.nemzetiszinhaz.hu

The focal point of a new "Millennium City Centre" in an inconvenient out-of-town site by the Danube, the lavish National Theatre is worth a look for its size, its weird mixture of styles, its brash statuary and its odd landscaping.

🚇 8Z ✉ Bajor Gizi Park 1, Budapest IX ☎ 476 6800 🚋 Tram: 1, 2, 24

VÁSÁRCSARNOK (CENTRAL MARKET HALL)

The Central Market Hall is full of the aromas of fresh vegetables, fish, hung sausages, cheeses and flowers, with beautiful folk art handicrafts. On the lower floor is the Pick Market, a mingling of modern supermarket and the bargain-basement stall. The best bargain is a beer and snack at one of the small bars on the upper floor.

🚇 5L ✉ Vámház körút 1–3, Budapest IX ☎ 366 3300
🕓 Mon 6am–5pm, Tue–Fri 6–6, Sat 6–3 ✋ Free 🚋 Tram: 2, 47, 49. Trolleybus: 83

HOTELS

Atlas City Hotel (€€)

In the heart of Józsefváros, this hotel looks fairly basic but its rooms are well-enough equipped and there's a bar on site. Blaha Lujza tér is a few minutes' walk away, as is Kerepes Cemetery (▶ 160).

✉ Népszínház utca 39–41, Budapest VIII ☎ 299 0256; www.atlashotelbudapest.com

Atrium (€€)

Conveniently located just off Blaha Lujza tér, this design hotel is based around an airy, contemporary-style atrium. Rooms are modern and spacious.

✉ Csokonai utca 14, Budapest VIII ☎ 299 0777; www.atriumhotelbudapest.com

Hotel Sissi (€€)

Aside from the antique-clad Sissi Room, reminders of the hotel's namesake – the much-beloved 19th-century Habsburg Empress Sissi – barely surface in this modern hotel. Rooms are spartan, clean and occasionally come with a balcony. The neighbourhood is quiet.

✉ Angyal utca 33, Budapest IX ☎ 215 0082; www.hotelsissi.hu

Ibis Centrum (€)

Just off the city centre and close to the shopping and business areas, this is a basic, affordable hotel. There's WiFi in all rooms, a 24-hour bar and the location is good.

✉ Ráday utca 6, Budapest IX ☎ 456 4100; www.ibis-centrum.hu

RESTAURANTS

Costes (€€€)

The fine Costes is Hungary's first Michelin-starred restaurant and it serves imaginative, highly accomplished international cuisine. You should allow a good three hours for dinner.

✉ Ráday utca 4, Budapest XI ☎ 219 0696; www.costes.hu 🕔 Wed–Sun 12–3:30, 6:30–12

Fülemüle (€€)

This lovely restaurant serves Jewish (but not kosher) cuisine. It specializes in goose, but also offers meat, fish and other poultry; vegetarians will have to settle for grilled cheese and salads.

✉ Kőfaragó utca 5, Budapest VIII ☎ 266 7947; www.fulemule.hu
🕐 Sun–Thu 12–10, Fri–Sat 12–11

Múzeum (€€)

See page 59.

Pata Negra (€€)

Order a bottle of Rioja and begin sampling from the selection of around 40 tapas here, or simply snack away on cheese and olives.

✉ Kálvin tér 8, Budapest IX ☎ 215 5616; www.patanegra.hu 🕐 Daily 11am–midnight

Pink Cadillac (€€)

Pink Cadillac isn't sophisticated, but it's fun. The menu selection – whether it be pizzas, pastas or salads – is extensive and the service quick and friendly.

✉ Ráday utca 22, Budapest IX ☎ 216 1412; www.pinkcadillac.hu
🕐 Mon–Fri 11am–midnight, Sat–Sun 12–12

Shiraz (€€)

Shiraz is a Persian restaurant on the bustling Ráday utca, where you can smoke a fruit-flavoured shisha sitting on beanbags on the floor upstairs. Try one of the many exotic teas.

✉ Ráday utca 21, Budapest IX ☎ 218 0881; www.shirazetterem.hu
🕐 Daily 12–12

CAFES

Café Csiga

Small Csiga is a proper locals' cafe, with a cosy ambience and eclectic decor. Choose from a stool at the bar or a table by the window. There's live music on Wednesdays.

✉ Vásár utca 2, Budapest VIII ☎ 210 0885; www.cafecsiga.org 🕐 Daily 11am–1am

Stex

More than a cafe, Stex welcomes with open arms those popping in for a drink, stopping for lunch or dinner, having a business meeting or on a night out. The set lunch menu is great value for money but the à-la-carte food is also inexpensive.

✉ József körút 55–57, Budapest VIII ☎ 318 5716; www.stexhaz.hu
🕐 Mon–Sat 8–4, Sun 9–2

SHOPPING

Babaház

Among the bars of Ráday utca, this shop sells handmade porcelain dolls dressed in costumes representing different eras. You can watch the creations come alive in the workshop.

✉ Ráday utca 14, Budapest IX ☎ 213 8295 🕐 Mon–Sat 12–8

Magyar Pálinka Háza

This store sells varieties of *pálinka*, Hungary's version of fruit brandy.

✉ Rákóczi út 17, Budapest VIII ☎ 338 4219; www.magyarpalinkahaza.hu
🕐 Mon–Sat 7–7

Vásárcsarnok

See page 165.

ENTERTAINMENT

NIGHTLIFE
Berliner Pub

This traditional-style beer hall has wooden benches, exposed brickwork and a big range of beers – including 35 Belgian brews. And if you want to enjoy your beer alfresco, there's also an outdoor terrace.

✉ Ráday utca 5, Budapest IX ☎ 217 6757; www.berliner.hu 🕐 Daily 12–12

Darshan Udvar

This collection of two bars, a cafe and a restaurant, all huddled around a North African-themed inner courtyard, is the heart of Krúdy utca's nightlife.

✉ Krúdy utca 7, Budapest VIII ☎ 266 5541; www.darshan.hu ◐ Daily
11am–midnight

Mojito
Mojito is a cheerful cocktail bar and cafe with polished wooden
floors and some street-side seating.
✉ Ráday utca 5, Budapest IX ☎ 215 4569; www.cafemojito.hu ◐ Mon–Sat
noon–1am

Trafó Bár Tangó
Filling the basement of the Trafó Kortárs Művészetek Háza
(► below), this long bar attracts an arty-party crowd with its
sleek look and locally renowned DJs, with jazz to alternative on
the turntables.
✉ Liliom utca 41, Budapest IX ☎ 456 2049; www.trafo.hu
◐ Daily 6pm–4am

LIVE ARTS
Művészetek Palotája
See pages 164–165.

Nemzeti Színház
See page 165.

Trafó Kortárs Művészetek Háza
(Trafó House of Contemporary Arts)
This former electrical transformer station hosts contemporary
performances including dance, theatre, music and readings.
✉ Liliom utca 41, Budapest IX ☎ 456 2040; www.trafo.hu ◐ Mon–Fri 2–8,
Sat–Sun 5–8

SPORT
Billiards
You can play billiards in almost 100 venues around the city, mainly
in pubs and clubs. The few dedicated billiard halls include:
Atlantis ✉ Váci út 156, Budapest XIII ☎ 349 4946; www.atlantisbiliard.hu
Black Pool ✉ Vámház körút 15, Budapest IX ☎ 218 9379

Excursions

City outskirts

Budai-hegyek (Buda Hills)   173–174

Szoborpark (Memento Park)   175

Further afield

Esztergom   176

Gödöllő   177

Szentendre   179

Visegrád   180–181

There's plenty to do beyond central Budapest. Easily reached by public transport are Memento Park and the Buda Hills, the first a display station for unwanted communist memorials, the second a string of wooded hills popular with walkers and cyclists. With a little more effort the pretty towns along the Danube to the north of Budapest can be explored. This stretch of the river is known as the Danube Bend, where rising hills have forced the river into sharp turns. Here you'll find Esztergom, birthplace of King Stephen I, Visegrád, with the ruins of King Matthias' medieval Royal Palace, and Szentendre, famous for its religious freedom and former artists' colony. Not far east of the capital is Gödöllő, home to an exceptional baroque palace built in the mid-18th century. Note that traffic out of the city can be heavy on Fridays, when many Pestians migrate to the countryside.

City outskirts

BUDAI-HEGYEK (BUDA HILLS)

The Buda Hills are Budapest's largest outdoor playground and stretch to well within the city's borders. They're not massive – the tallest peaks are just over 500m (1,640ft) – but they offer a quick escape from urban living and a chance to breathe clean, fresh air. And with a few quirky transport choices, getting there is half the fun. Two tram stops from Buda's Moszkva tér is the Fogaskerekű vasút (Cog Railway), a fun but occasionally jarring way up into the hills. When completed in 1874, it ran on steam. For the best views, sit on the right-hand side facing backwards. The railway is included in the city's transport tickets.

Only a short walk from the Cog Railway's final stop is another unusual railway, the Gyermekvasút (Children's Railway, ➤ 62). This narrow-gauge rail was built in 1948 by the socialist version of the Scouts and is still run almost solely by enthusiastic children between the ages of 10 and 14. The dinky little train winds its way through wooded hills to Hűvösvölgy, about 12km (7.5 miles) from its starting point (40-minute journey). Disembark at János-hegy for Erzsébet-kilátó (Elisabeth Tower), the hill's highest point at 527m (1,876ft), and yet another unusual transport option, the **libegő** (chairlift, ➤ 63).

One of the few museums in the hills is the **Bartók Béla Emlékház** (Béla Bartók Memorial House), devoted to one of Hungary's greatest musicians.

🚌 Trams 18 and 56 from Moszkva tér (on the M2 line) lead directly into the Buda Hills and call at the Cog Railway en route

Libegő

✉ Jánoshegyi/Zugligeti út

🕐 Mid-May to mid-Sep daily 10–5; mid-Sep to mid-May 10–3:30

✋ Inexpensive

Bartók Béla Emlékház

✉ Csalán út 29 ☎ 394 2100; www.bartokmuseum.hu

🕐 Tue–Sun 10–5 ✋ Moderate

SZOBORPARK (MEMENTO PARK)

The former "Statue Park" is home to more than 40 statues that graced the cityscape during the communist era. It is a popular – and surreal – attraction on the outskirts of Budapest.

Enormous statues of Lenin, Marx and Engels greet visitors to the park. Inside, the remaining 39 statues are laid out in semi-circles, and almost all are a uniform dark grey, with patches of pale green where the metal's outer shell has worn thin. Easily the most impressive statue is Imre Varga's Béla Kun memorial (statue No 24); this bronze, copper and steel piece shows Kun directing soldiers into the fray. Other striking examples include the massive – and powerful – Republics of Councils monument (statue No 33) and the memorial to the Hungarian freedom fighters who fought in the Spanish Civil War (statue No 32).

Despite their intended purpose, other statues appear almost comical; a cricket fielder stretches for a spectacular catch (Martyrs monument, statue No 38) and a lollipop man prepares to stop traffic at a pedestrian crossing (Osztapenkó, statue No 41). The park's shop sells bizarre Soviet souvenirs such as Lenin and Stalin candles, communist pocket watches and Best of Communism CDs.

www.mementopark.hu

✉ Corner of Balatoni út and Szabadkai utca, Budapest XXII

☎ 424 7500 🕓 Daily 10am–sunset 💷 Expensive

🚌 Direct bus services run from the corner of V. Deák Ferenc tér and Harmincad utca. Cheaper buses leave from Etele tér, Budapest XI: catch a yellow Volán bus from stand 7 to Diósd-Érd and ask the driver to let you off at the park

Further afield

ESZTERGOM

Birthplace of King Stephen I, this is one of Hungary's most historically important and fascinating cities. Its history dates back to Roman times. Sadly, much of the original city was destroyed by the Turks in 1543. All the same, it boasts some of Hungary's most prestigious buildings, the most impressive of which is the Basilika, Hungary's largest cathedral. Little remains of the medieval building, with the present neoclassical structure dating from the early 19th century. The Bakócz Chapel is by far the most dominant feature in this sumptuously decorated building. The white marble altar is the work of Florentine craftsmen and was designed by Andreas Ferrucci in 1519. With its many priceless medieval objects, including the 13th-century Hungarian Coronation Cross, the treasury is also the resting place of Cardinal Mindszenty, the cathedral's best-known clergyman, and a leading critic of the communist regime. Beside the basilica is the Vár Múzeum (Castle Museum), housing the fascinating remains of the former royal palace.

Don't miss the Keresztény Múzeum (Christian Museum), containing the best collection of medieval religious art in Hungary, as well as works by Italian masters Duccio, Lorenzo di Credi and Giovanni di Paola. Since the Danube is such a dominant feature of the town, there's the Duna Múzeum (Danube Museum) to help you understand its evolution. Although most of the captions at this museum are in Hungarian, this doesn't lessen the impact of the exhibition.

🚌 Frequent service from Budapest's Árpád híd bus station 🚆 Regular service from Nyugati Railway Station ❓ By car: 66km (41 miles), route 10, then 111 ℹ️ Gran Tours, Széchenyi tér 25, Esztergom; tel: (33) 502 001

GÖDÖLLŐ

An easy trip by car or suburban train, this small town is dominated by the great **baroque palace** begun in 1741 by Empress Maria Theresa's favourite courtier, Count Grassalkovich. It is claimed to be outdone in size only by the Palace of Versailles in France, but visitors come here less for architectural pomp than for the palace's associations with another empress, Franz Joseph's consort Elisabeth. "Sissi", as she was known, fell in love with all things Hungarian, and was loved in return. The palace has been largely restored after use in communist times as an old people's home; Sissi fans will find much evidence of her presence here, though few of the furnishings and fittings are original. An exception is the completely intact baroque theatre, a real rarity. You can walk in the palace's park, dress up as a Habsburg and have your photo taken, or browse the range of superior souvenirs in the gift shop.

Gödöllő was also attractive to artists, and a century ago a utopian artistic colony was formed here, its members coming from as far away as Paris. The **town museum** has good examples of their work and nicely evokes their earnest, bearded and sandalled way of life. Gödöllő may be far from the *puszta*, but you can admire spectacular horsemanship at the **Lázár Equestrian Park** nearby, where the traditional atmosphere of the Hungarian countryside has been carefully re-created.

Royal Palace

✉ Grassalkovich Kastély, 2100 Gödöllő ☎ (28) 410 124; www.kiralyikastely.hu
🕐 Apr–Oct daily 10–6; Nov–Mar 10–5 💰 Expensive 🍴 Cafe (€–€€)
🚇 Frequent HÉV suburban trains from Örs vezér tere (terminus of Metro line 2) to Gödöllő Szabadság tér station ❓ By car: 30km (18.6 miles), M3 motorway

Gödöllő town museum

✉ Szabadság tér 5, 2100 Gödöllő ☎ (28) 422 002 🕐 Mar–Oct Tue–Sun 10–6; Nov–Feb 10–4 💰 Inexpensive

Lázár Equestrian Park

✉ Lázár Lóvaspark, 2182 Gödöllő-Domonyvölgy ☎ (28) 576 510; www.lazarlovaspark.hu. Call to check times of shows 🍴 Dining halls (€–€€)
❓ By car: 5km (3 miles) east of Gödöllő, route 3

SZENTENDRE

Szentendre lies in a beautiful vale of hills beside the Danube. Founded in the 11th century, it takes its name from the guardian angel of its church, András (Endre). In the 14th century it became a royal estate, but 150 years of Turkish occupation followed, during which the town was virtually deserted. It was later settled by rich Serbian and Dalmatian craftsmen and merchants, but the town again went into decline. But much is still intact, and it's worth starting your visit on Fő tér (Main Square), with its huddled houses and alleyways like Jenő Dumsta utca and Bogdány utca, the main shopping and restaurant area. The Memorial Cross in the middle of the square was erected in thanks for the end of the Black Death by the Privileged Merchants' Company in 1763.

Nearby is the Orthodox Episcopal Church, also known as Beograda. Built between 1756 and 1764, its baroque architecture houses an ornamented and decorated interior. The splendid Margit Kovács Museum is one of the most delightful galleries in Szentendre and houses the works of the famous ceramicist after whom it is named. For superb views of the town, and a pleasant walk as well, take a stroll up to Templom tér, Szentendre's highest point, where a narrow cobbled lane leads up to the square. From here you'll be treated to a cavalcade of russet roof tiles sloping down to the Danube, interrupted by dots of green gardens. No trip to the town of Szentendre would be complete without a visit to the fascinating Szabadtéri Néprajzi Múzeum (Open-air Museum of the Hungarian Village). Originals of houses, buildings and machines were reassembled here to represent the country's vernacular architecture.

🚆 HÉV train: From Budapest's Batthyány tér station every 20–30 minutes
🚌 From Budapest's Újpest Városkapu station; takes 30 minutes
🚢 Mar–Oct. Contact Mahart PassNave; tel: 484 4013; www.mahartpassnave.hu ❓ By car: 20km (12.5 miles), route 11

VISEGRÁD

Offering magnificent views of the Danube, Visegrád (a Slav name meaning "lofty fortress") lies on the river's abrupt loop between the Pilis and Börzsöny hills. The town dates from Roman times, when the Danube formed the border of the Roman Empire. After the Mongol invasion, the Hungarian kings built the imposing citadel dominating the hilltop above Solomon's Tower. During the Turkish occupation Visegrád was virtually destroyed, and later the Habsburgs blew up the citadel to prevent its use by Hungarian independence fighters. Now undergoing restoration, the best way to reach it is by the excellent hiking trails, following signposts marked "Fellegvár", starting from behind the Catholic church.

The other major sight worth looking at in Visegrád is the 14th-century Royal Palace. Largely destroyed by the Habsburgs in 1702, the building has been under excavation since 1934, and its Gothic terraces have been reconstructed. Highlights here include replicas of the red-marbled Hercules Fountain in the Gothic courtyard and the Lion Fountain.

🚊 Regular return service from Budapest's Újpest Városkapu station

🚆 Services run to Szob (24 daily) from Budapest-Nyugati station. Get off at Nagymaros-Visegrád and take a ferry across to Visegrád 🚢 Mahart hydrofoil links Budapest and Esztergom via Visegrád; see www.mahartpassnave.hu for times and prices ❓ By car: 40km (25 miles), route 11 ℹ️ Visegrád Tours, Rév utca 15; tel: (26) 398 160

RESTAURANTS

BUDAI-HEGYEK
Origo Bisztro (€€)
A stylish modern bistro with a minimalist design, Origo Bisztro
serves international food and offers some good set-price menus.
There's also an adjacent cafe.

✉ Pasaréti tér, Budapest II ☎ 376 6039; www.origobisztro.hu ⏰ Cafe: daily
7:30am–midnight. Bistro: Mon–Fri 12–12, Sat–Sun 10am–midnight

Udvarház Restaurant (€€)
Twenty minutes from the city centre, on top of Hármashatár-hegy,
this restaurant has breathtaking views of the city. It's slightly
difficult to reach – you're best to go by car. In high season, there's
gypsy music and a folklore programme every night.

✉ Hármashatár-hegyi út 2, Budapest III ☎ 388 8780; www.udvarhaz.hu
⏰ Apr–Oct daily 12–11; Nov–Mar Wed–Fri 3–11, Sat–Sun 12–11

ESZTERGOM
Csülök Csárda (€)
Home-style Hungarian cooking and pork knuckles are the
specialities of this pleasant restaurant, with its summer terrace.

✉ Batthyány Lajos utca 9 ☎ (33) 412 420; www.csulokcsarda.hu
⏰ Daily 12–10

Mélytányér (€€)
Large portions of traditional Hungarian and international dishes are
served here. There's a garden and the service is friendly.

✉ Pázmány Péter utca 1 ☎ (33) 412 534; www.melytanyer.hu
⏰ Daily 12–9:30

Padlizsán (€€€)
A little further up the same road as Mélytányér, this restaurant, in
a former peasant farm building, is more upmarket. There are three-
course set-lunch menus and à-la-carte dinners. You can enjoy
views over the basilica from the courtyard.

✉ Pázmány Péter utca 21 ☎ (33) 322 212; www.padlizsanetterem.hu
⏰ Daily 12–12

SZENTENDRE
Aranysárkány (€€)
Family-run Aranysárkány serves fine Hungarian and Austrian cuisine. There's an open kitchen and a large wine selection.

✉ Alkotmány utca 1/a ☎ (26) 301 479; www.aranysarkany.hu 🕒 Daily 12–10

Promenade (€€)
Closer to the river, this pleasant restaurant has a mix of Hungarian and international dishes, and a large, breezy terrace.

✉ Futó utca 4 ☎ (26) 312 626; www.promenade-szentendre.hu 🕒 Daily 12–10

Rab Ráby (€€)
Medieval knight armour and weapons cover the wall here. It's very touristy, serving Hungarian dishes, and some Serbian. For a meat overload, order the Rab Raby wooden plate for two people.

✉ Kucsera Ferenc utca 1/a ☎ (26) 310 819; www.rabraby.hu 🕒 Daily 12–11

Szamos Cukrászda (€)
Choose from a range of cakes, bonbons and pastries, to eat in or take away. Then visit the marzipan museum next door.

✉ Dumtsa Jenő utca 12 ☎ (26) 310 545; www.szamosmarcipan.hu 🕒 Daily 10–7

VISEGRÁD
Nagyvillám Vadászcsárda (€€€)
Directly underneath the Fellegvár, this restaurant specializes in dishes of game and wild mushroom. The views over the castle and the Danube Bend are worth the trek up here.

✉ Nagyvillám ☎ (26) 398 070; www.nagyvillam.hu 🕒 Mon–Wed 12–4, Fri–Sun 12–dusk

Sirály (€€)
A large, modern restaurant on the bank of the Danube, the Sirály offers Hungarian and international cuisine. In the summer, try to snatch a table on the terrace, overlooking the river.

✉ Rév utca 15 ☎ (26) 398 376; www.siralyvisegrad.hu 🕒 Daily 12–12

Index

Academy of Music 71, 141
accommodation see hotels
air travel 26
Állatkert 62, 71, 146–147
Amusement Park 63, 147
Andrássy út 19, 65, 138
Andrássy Avenue 19, 65, 138
Applied Arts Museum 71, 162
Aquincum 74, 94
Arany Sas Patikamúzeum 76
Árpád Bridge 94–95
Árpád híd 94–95
art nouveau 71, 115, 122–123
ATMs 30

banks 30, 32
Bartók, Béla 174
Bartók Béla Emlékház 174
Bécsi Kapu 76–77
Bedő Ház 71
Béla Bartók Memorial House
    174
Belváros and Lipótváros
    115–136
    cafes 129–130
    entertainment 135–136
    hotels 126–127
    restaurants 127–129
    shopping 130–135
    sights 116–125
Belvárosi Plébániatemplom
    116–117
billiards 169
Blaha Lujza tér 65
Buda 10, 74
Buda Royal Palace 19, 36–37
Buda Hills 173–174
Budavári Labirintus 77
Budapest History Museum 37,
    78
Budapest Puppet Theatre 62
Budapesti Bábszínház 62
Budapesti Történeti Múzeum
    37, 78
Budai Királyi Palota 19, 36–37
buses
    city 28
    long-distance 27

cafes 101–102, 129–130,
    154–155, 167–168
car rental 29
Castle Hill 17, 54–55, 68, 90–91
Castle Labyrinth 77
Castle Theatre 88

Cave Church 109
Central Market Hall 165
Chairlift 63, 174
children's entertainment 62–63,
    104, 146–147
Children's Railway 62, 174
Christian Museum 176
church opening hours 32
churches
    Cave Church 109
    Ferencváros Parish Church
        64
    Inner City Parish Church
        116–117
    Mary Magdalene Tower 54,
        82–83
    Matthias Church 19, 46–47
    St Anne's Church 93
    St Stephen's Basilica 50–51,
        68
circus 62
Citadel 39, 106
Citadella 39, 106
City Park 146–147
climate 22
Cog Railway 173
credit cards 30
crime 32
Csodák Palotája: Interaktív
    Tudományos Játszóház 62

Danube Promenade 117
Deer House 112
drinking water 31
driving 22, 26, 29
Dunakorzó 68, 117

eating out see restaurants
economy 11
electricity 32
Elisabeth, Empress (statue) 110
embassies and consulates 31
entertainment
    Belváros and Lipótváros
        135–136
    Gellért-hegy and the Tabán
        114
    Józsefváros and Ferencváros
        168–169
    Terézváros, Erzsébetváros
        and Városliget 156–158
    Vár-hegy, Víziváros and
        Óbuda 88
Erzsébet királyné szobor 110
Esztergom 176

Eugene of Savoy (statue) 36, 80
Europe Grove 77
excursions 170–183
    Budai-hegyek 173–174
    Esztergom 176
    Gödöllő 177
    restaurants 182–183
    Szoborpark 175
    Szentendre 179
    Visegrád 180–181

Ferenc Hopp Museum of
    Eastern Asiatic Art 138
Ferenc Liszt Memorial
    Museum 138–139
Ferencváros Parish Church 64
ferries and hydrofoils 27
festivals and events 24–25
Fine Arts Museum 52–53
Fishermen's Bastion 16, 40–41
Földalatti Vasúti Múzeum 118
Földtani Intézet 71
food and drink 12–15
    drinking water 31
    Hungarian cuisine 12–14
    wines, beers and spirits
        14–15
    see also restaurants
Former Royal Post Office
    Savings Bank 71, 123
Fortuna utca 91
Foundry Museum 93
Fővárosi Nagycirkusz 62
Freedom Bridge 108–109
Funicular 63, 84

Gellért Emlékmű 106
Gellért Hill 17, 38–39, 68
Gellért Hotel 107–108
Gellért Monument 106
Gellért Thermal Baths 71,
    107–108
Gellért-hegy 17, 38–39, 68
Gellért-hegy and the Tabán
    105–114
    entertainment 114
    hotels 113
    restaurants 113–114
    sights 106–112
geography 11
Geology Institute 71
Gödöllő 177
Golden Eagle Pharmacy 76
Grand Boulevard 64–65
Great Plain 11

Great Synagogue 142
Gresham Palace 71, 122–123
Gundel Étterem 147
Gundel Restaurant 147
Gyermekvasút 62, 174

Hadtörténeti Múzeum 82
Halászbástya 16, 40–41
health 22, 23, 31
Hercules Villa 95
Heroes' Square 148–149
Holocaust Memorial 142
Holocaust Museum 162
Holokauszt Emlékközpont 162
Holy Trinity Column 86
Hopp Ferenc Kelet-ázsiai Múzeum 138
Hősök tere 148–149
Hotel Gellért és Gellért Gyógyfürdő 107–108
hotels
  Belváros and Lipótváros 126–127
  Gellért-hegy and the Tabán 113
  Józsefváros and Ferencváros 166
  Terézváros, Erzsébetváros and Városliget 150–151
  Vár-hegy, Víziváros and Óbuda 96–98
House of Terror 140–141
Hungarian Academy of Sciences 123–124
Hungarian Museum of Tourism and Trade 118
Hungarian National Gallery 36, 41, 79
Hungarian National Museum 160–161
Hungarian Natural History Museum 161
Hungarian State Opera House 42–43

Inner City Parish Church 116–117
insurance 22, 23
internet services 31
Iparművészeti Múzeum 71, 162

János-hegy 68
Jewish District 137, 142

Józsefváros and Ferencváros 159–169
  cafes 167–168
  entertainment 168–169
  hotels 166
  restaurants 166–167
  shopping 168
  sights 160–165

Kerepesi Cemetery 160
Keresztény Múzeum 176
Király Gyógyfürdő 92
Király Thermal Baths 92
Klemperer, Otto 43
Közlekedési Múzeum 149

language 11, 33
Lázár Equestrian Park 177
Libegő 63, 174
Liberation Monument 39,109
Liberty Bridge 39
Liberty Square 125
Liszt, Franz 138–139, 141
Liszt Ferenc Emlékmúzeum 138–139
Lords' Street 88
Ludwig Museum Budapest 164–165

Magyar Állami Operaház 42–43
Magyar Kereskedelmi és Vendéglátóipari Múzeum 118
Magyar Királyi Posta Takarékpénztár 71, 123
Magyar Nemzeti Galéria 36, 41, 79
Magyar Nemzeti Múzeum 160–161
Magyar Természettudományi Múzeum 161
Magyar Tudományos Akadémia 123–124
Mahler, Gustav 43
Margaret Island 19, 44–45
Margit Kovács Museum 179
Margitsziget 19, 44–45
Mária Magdolna-torony 54, 82–83
Mary Magdalene Tower 54, 82–83
Matthias Church 19, 46–47
Matthias Well 36, 79–80
Mátyás-kút 36, 79–80
Mátyás-templom 19, 46–47
medical treatment 23

Metro 28
Miksa Róth Memorial House 143
Millennium Monument 148–149
money 30
Mulberry Garden 145
Municipal Circus 62
Municipal Zoo 62, 71, 146–147
museum opening hours 32
museums and galleries
  Applied Arts Museum 71, 162
  Béla Bartók Memorial House 174
  Budapest History Museum 37, 78
  Christian Museum 176
  Ferenc Hopp Museum of Eastern Asiatic Art 138
  Ferenc Liszt Memorial Museum 138–139
  Fine Arts Museum 52–53
  Foundry Museum 93
  Golden Eagle Pharmacy 76
  Holocaust Museum 162
  Hungarian Museum of Tourism and Trade 118
  Hungarian National Gallery 36, 41, 79
  Hungarian National Museum 160–161
  Hungarian Natural History Museum 161
  Ludwig Múzeum Budapest 164–165
  Margit Kovács Museum 179
  Miksa Róth Memorial House 143
  Museum of Ethnography 124–125
  Museum of Medical History 112
  Museum of Military History 82
  Open-air Museum of the Hungarian Village 179
  Postal Museum 140
  Ráth György Múzeum 138
  Telephone Museum 86
  Transport Museum 149
  Underground Railway Museum 118

Nagy zsinagóga 142
Nagykörút 64–65
National Archives of Hungary 91
National Dance Theatre 104
national holidays 24
National Széchényi Library
    36–37, 80
National Theatre 165
Nernzeti Színház 165
Néprajzi Múzeum 124–125
New York Café 143
New York Kávéház 143
nightlife 103–104, 114,
    135–136, 156–158, 168–169
Nyugati Pályaudvar 139–140

Old Town Hall 84
Öntödei Múzeum 93
Open-air Museum of the
    Hungarian Village 179
opening hours 32
Országház 17, 48–49
Országház utca 83
Országos Széchényi Könyvtár
    36–37, 80

Palace of Arts 164
Palace of Miracles: Interactive
    Scientific Playhouse 62
Parliament 17, 48–49
passports and visas 22
personal safety 32
Pest 10, 74, 115, 137
pharmacies 31, 32
Planetárium 63
police 32
Postal Museum 140
postal services 31
Postamúzeum 140
Procession Square 149
public transport 28–29

Rákóczi tér 64
Ráth György Múzeum 138
Régi Budai Városháza 84
restaurants 58–59
    Belváros and Lipótváros
        127–129
    Excursions 182–183
    Gellért-hegy and the Tabán
        113–114
    Józsefváros and Ferencváros
        166–167
    Terézváros, Erzsébetváros
        and Városliget 151–154

Vár-hegy, Víziváros and
    Óbuda 98–101
river boats 28
River Danube 11, 180
Róth, Miksa 143
Róth Miksa Emlékház 143
Rudas Gyógyfürdő 39, 110
Rudas Thermal Baths 39, 110
Ruszwurm pastry shop 54–55,
    102

St Stephen's Basilica 50–51, 68
Savoyai Jenő szobor 36, 80
Schulek, Frigyes 40, 46
Semmelweis Orvostörténeti
    Múzeum 112
shopping
    Belváros and Lipótváros
        130–135
    Józsefváros and Ferencváros
        168
    opening hours 32
    Terézváros, Erzsébetváros
        and Városliget 155–156
    Vár-hegy, Víziváros and
        Óbuda 102–103
Sikló 63, 84
sport 104, 169
Statue Park 175
sun safety 31
Szabadság híd 108–109
Szabadság szobor 109
Szabadság tér 125
Szarvas-ház 112
Széchenyi Chain Bridge 84–85
Széchenyi Gyógyfürdő 147
Széchenyi Lánchíd 84–85
Szent Anna Templom 93
Szent István Bazilika 50–51, 68
Szentendre 179
Szentháromsag szobor 86
Szépművészeti Múzeum 52–53
Sziklatemplom 109
Szoborpark 175

taxis 29
telephones 31
Telephónia Múzeum 86
Terézváros, Erzsébetváros and
    Városliget 137–158
    cafes 154–155
    entertainment 156–158
    hotels 150–151
    restaurants 151–154
    shopping 155–156

sights 138–149
Terror Háza 140–141
theatre 104, 136, 158
thermal baths 19, 66–67, 92,
    107–108, 110, 147
Thonet Ház 71
time differences 23
Tomb of the Unknown Soldier
    149
Török Bankház 71
tourist information 23, 30
train services 26, 28
trams 28
Transport Museum 149
traveller's cheques 30
travelling to Budapest 26–27
Turkish Bank House 71

Underground Railway Museum
    118
Úri utca 88

Váci utca 119
Vár-hegy 17, 54–55, 68, 90–91
Vár-hegy, Víziváros and Óbuda
    75–104
    cafes 101–102
    entertainment 103–104
    hotels 96–98
    restaurants 98–101
    shopping 102–103
    sights 76–95
Városliget 146–147
Várszínház 88
Vásárcsarnok 165
VI District 144–145
Vidámpark 63, 147
Vienna Gate 76–77
views of Budapest 68
Visegrád 180–181
Vörösmarty tér 17, 119

walks
    Inner City 120–121
    Nagykörút (Grand Boulevard)
        64–65
    Vár-hegy (Castle Hill) 90–91
    VI District 144–145
War Memorial 64
websites 23
Western Railway Station
    139–140

Zeneakadémia 141
zoo 62, 71, 146–147

Street index

Aba utca **8N**
Abonyi utca **11R**
Ady Endre utca **1E**
Áfonya utca **1C**
Ág utca **1J**
Ajtósi Dürer sor **11Q**
Akácfa utca **7S**
Akadémia utca **4G**
Alagút utca **2J**
Alföldi utca **9U**
Alkotás utca **1K**
Alkotmány utca **4F**
Állatkerti körút **9N**
Almássy utca **8S**
Alpár utca **10S**
Alsó erdősor utca **9S**
Alsóhegy utca **1M**
Alsó Zöldmáli út **1B**
Amerikai út **12P**
Andrássy út **8R**
Angyalföldi út **6B**
Angyal utca **8X**
Apáczai Csere János
utca **4J**
Apály utca **6B**
Apáthy István utca **9W**
Ápolka utca **1C**
Apostol utca **2D**
Aradi utca **8Q**
Arany János utca **4H**
Aranykéz utca **4J**
Árboc utca **6A**
Árpád Fejedelem útja
3D
Asztalos Sándor út **12T**
Attila út **1H**
Aulich utca **4G**
Auróra utca **9U**
Avar utca **1K**
Babits M sétány **2G**
Bácskai utca **12P**
Bacsó Béla utca **8T**
Bajcsy Zsilinszky út **5G**
Bajmóczi utca **1M**
Bajnok utca **7Q**
Bajvívó utca **1F**
Bajza utca **9Q**
Bakator utca **2M**
Bakáts tér **7W**
Bakáts utca **7W**
Balassa utca **10W**
Balassi Bálint utca **4F**
Balaton utca **4F**
Balázs Béla utca **9X**
Balzac utca **4D**

Bank utca **4G**
Bán utca **1K**
Barát utca **8T**
Barcsay utca **8S**
Bárd utca **9Y**
Baross utca **9V**
Barsi utca **1E**
Bartók Béla út **4M**
Bástya utca **5L**
Báthory utca **5G**
Batsányi utca **11X**
Batthyány utca **2G**
Bécsi utak **2B**
Bécsi utca **4J**
Belgrád rakpart **4J**
Bem József utca **2E**
Bem rakpart **3E**
Benczúr köz **9Q**
Benczúr utca **9Q**
Beniczky Lajos utca
9V
Benyovszky Móric utca
11X
Bérc utca **3L**
Berkenye utca **1D**
Bérkocsis utca **8U**
Berzenczey utca **8X**
Berzsenyi utca **9T**
Bessenyei utca **5C**
Bethesda utca **10N**
Bethlen Gábor tér **9R**
Bethlen Gábor utca **9R**
Bezerédj utca **8T**
Bihari János utca **5F**
Bimbó utak **1E**
Biró Lajos utca **11W**
Bláthy Ottó utca **12X**
Bókay János utca **9W**
Bokor utca **2A**
Bokréta utca **8X**
Bólyai utca **1D**
Borbolya utca **2D**
Boróka utca **1B**
Botond utca **6C**
Bródy Sándor utca **7U**
Budafoki út **5M**
Budai alsó rakpart **3G**
Budaörsi út **1M**
Buday László utca **2E**
Bugát utca **1H**
Bulcsú utca **6D**
Cerje utca **1C**
Cházár András utca
10R
Citad utca **3M**

Clark Ádám tér **3H**
Csalogány utca **2F**
Csanády utca **5D**
Csángó utca **6B**
Csányi utca **7S**
Csarnok tér **5L**
Csejtei köz **1C**
Csejtei utca **1C**
Csengery utca **8R**
Cserei utca **12R**
Cserfa utca **1C**
Cserhát utca **10R**
Csetneki utca **2M**
Csobánc utca **11V**
Csokonai utca **8T**
Csörsz utca **1K**
Cukor utca **5K**
Czakó utca **2K**
Czuczor utca **6L**
Dalszínház utca **5G**
Damjanich utca **9R**
Dandár utca **8Y**
Dankó utca **10U**
Darázs utca **2C**
Daru utca **2B**
Deák Ferenc utca **4J**
Delej utca **11X**
Délibáb utca **9Q**
Dembinszky utca **9R**
Deregye utca **3A**
Derék utca **2K**
Déri Miksa utca **8U**
Dessewffy utca **5K**
Dévai utca **7N**
Dezso utca **2K**
Diószeghy Sámeul
utca **11W**
Dísz tér **2H**
Dobozi utca **10U**
Dob utca **7S**
Dohány utca **8S**
Dologház utca **10T**
Donáti utca **2G**
Dorottya utca **4J**
Dorozsmai utca **11N**
Dózsa György út **10Q**
Dráva utca **5B**
Drégely utca **8Y**
Dugonics utca **10W**
Duna utca **5K**
Dvorák sétány **10Q**
Egressy út **12R**
Elek utca **2M**
Elnök utca **11X**
Eötvös tér **4H**

Eötvös utca **6F**
Erdélyi utca **9U**
Erkel utca **6L**
Ernő utca **10X**
Erőd utca **2F**
Erzsébet hid **4K**
Erzsébet királyné útja
11N
Erzsébet körút **8S**
Erzsébet tér **4H**
Esztergomi út **6A**
Eszter utca **1D**
Evező utca **3B**
Fajd utca **1C**
Falk Miksa utca **4F**
Fazekas utca **2F**
Fecske utca **9U**
Fejér György utca **5K**
Fekete Sas utca **2E**
Fék utca **11Z**
Felhévizi utca **2B**
Felső erdősor utca **8Q**
Felvonulási tér **10Q**
Fém utca **2K**
Fényes Elek utca **1F**
Fenyő utca **2J**
Fény utca **1F**
Ferdinánd hid **6E**
Ferenc körút **8W**
Ferenc tér **8X**
Ferenczy István utca
5K
Festetics György utca
10T
Feszty Árpád utca **1H**
Fiáth J utca **1G**
Fiumei út **10U**
Folyóka utca **1A**
Folyondár köz **1A**
Folyondár utca **1A**
Fő utca **3H**
Fővám tér **5L**
Francia út **11P**
Frankel Leó út **2D**
Franklin utca **2G**
Füge utca **1E**
Futó utca **9W**
Füvészkert utca **10V**
Gabona utca **8X**
Galagonya utca **3A**
Galamb utca **4J**
Gálya utca **7W**
Ganz utca **2F**
Garam utca **5C**
Garay utca **10S**

Garibaldi utca **4G**
Gát utca **9X**
Gázláng utca **9T**
Gellérthegy utca **2J**
Gerlóczy utca **5J**
Gizella sétány **8Y**
Gizella út **12Q**
Gogol utca **5C**
Goldmann György tér
7X
Golgota utca **12W**
Gönczy Pál utca **5L**
Gőzmalom utca **8Z**
Gül Baba utca **2D**
Gutenberg tér **8U**
Gyáli utca **11Y**
Gyarmat utca **12P**
Gyorffy István utca
12X
Gyori útak **1K**
Gyorskocsi utca **2F**
Győző utca **1J**
Gyukai Pál utca **8T**
Hajós Alfréd sétány **4B**
Hajós utca **5G**
Haller utca **8Y**
Haris köz **5K**
Hársfa utca **8S**
Hattyú utca **1F**
Havas utca **5K**
Hegedus Gyula utca
5D
Hegyalja útak **2K**
Henszimann Imre utca
5K
Hercegprímás utca **4H**
Hermina út **11P**
Hernád utca **10R**
Herzl Tivadar tér **5J**
Hevesi Sándor tér **8R**
Hild tér **4H**
Hock János utca **9V**
Hogyes Endre utca **8W**
Hold utca **4G**
Holdvilág utca **1M**
Hollán Erno utca **4E**
Holló utca **5H**
Homok utca **9U**
Honvéd utca **4F**
Horánszky utca **8U**
Horváth Mihály tér **9V**
Horvát utca **2F**
Huba utca **6B**
Hunfalvy utca **2G**
Hungária körút **11P**

Hunyadi János út **2H**
Hunyadi tér **8R**
Huszár utca **9S**
Ida utca **11Q**
Iglói utca **3L**
Ilka utca **11Q**
Illés köz **10W**
Illés utca **10V**
Imre utca **6L**
Ipar utca **8X**
Ipoly utca **5D**
Irányi utca **5K**
Iskola utca **2G**
István út **9R**
Istvánmezei út **11S**
Izabella utca **8R**
Izsó utca **11R**
Janicsár utca **6A**
Jávor utca **11Q**
Jázmin utca **9W**
Jobbágy utca **10S**
Jókai utca **5F**
Jósika utca **8R**
Jószerencse utca **1A**
József Attila utca **4H**
József körút **8V**
Józsefhegyi út **1C**
József nádor tér **4H**
József utca **8U**
Jurányi utca **3H**
Kacsa utca **2F**
Kádár utca **5E**
Kagyló utca **2G**
Kálmán Imre utca **4G**
Kálvária tér **10V**
Kálvária utca **10V**
Kálvin tér **6K**
Kapás utca **2F**
Kapucinus utca **3H**
Karácsony Sándor utca **10U**
Karolina út **1M**
Károlyi Mihály utca **5K**
Károly körút **5J**
Kárpát utca **5C**
Kassák Lajos utca **7N**
Katona József utca **4E**
Kavics utca **2C**
Kazinczy utca **6H**
Kecske utca **2A**
Kelenhegyi út **3M**
Keleti Károly utca **1E**
Kemenes utca **4M**
Kerepesi út **11S**
Kereszt utca **3K**
Kertész utca **7S**
Kígyó utca **5K**
Kilátás utca **2B**
Kinizsi utca **7W**

Királyi Pál utca **5K**
Király utca **8R**
Kis Diófa utca **6H**
Kisfaludy utca **8V**
Kis Fuvaros utca **9U**
Kisrókus utca **1E**
Kiss János altábornagy utca **1J**
Kiss József utca **9T**
Kitaibel Pál utca **1E**
Klauzál utca **7T**
Klauzál tér **7S**
Kmety György utca **8Q**
Knézits utca **8W**
Kobányai út **12V**
Köbölkút utca **2M**
Kocsány utca **3L**
Kőfaragó utca **8U**
Kolosy tér **3B**
Kolozsvári T utca **2B**
Kolumbusz utca **11N**
Komjádi Béla utca **2C**
Komor M utca **8Z**
Könyves kálmán körút **12Y**
Korányi Sándor utca **10W**
Koris utca **10V**
Korlát utca **1H**
Korong utca **12P**
Kosciuszkó Tádé utca **1J**
Kós Károly sétány **10P**
Kossuth Lajos utca **5J**
Kossuth Lajos tér **4F**
Koszorú utca **9U**
Kozet utca **1A**
Kozma Ferenc utca **4G**
Közraktár utca **6M**
Köztársaság tér **9T**
Köztelek utca **7V**
Kresz Géza utca **5E**
Kristal köz **8W**
Krisztina körút **3K**
Krúdy utca **8V**
Kun utca **9U**
Kuny Domonkos utca **1J**
Kürt utca **7S**
Kút utca **2E**
Lágymányosi híd **7Z**
Lajos utca **2B**
Laky Adolf utca **12N**
Lánchíd utca **3J**
Latorca utca **5A**
Lechner Ödön fasor **8Y**
Légszesz utca **9T**
Lehel utca **7N**
Lendvay utca **8P**

Lenhossék utca **9X**
Lenke köz **11Z**
Lenkey utca **11Z**
Leonardo da Vinci utca **9W**
Levél utca **1D**
Liliom utca **8X**
Lipthay utca **3E**
Lisznyai utca **2J**
Liszt Ferenc tér **7R**
Livia utca **1A**
Logodi utca **1H**
Lónyai utca **6L**
Loportár utca **8N**
Lósy Imre utca **9W**
Lovag utca **5G**
Lóvásár utca **10T**
Lovassy László utca **9U**
Lovas út **1G**
Lövőház utca **1F**
Lövölde tér **8R**
Lublói utca **2B**
Ludovika tér **10W**
Lujza utca **10U**
Luther utca **9T**
Magdolna utca **9V**
Magyar tudósok körútja **7Z**
Magyar utca **6K**
Mandula utca **1D**
Mányoki út **4M**
Március 15 tér **4K**
Marek József utca **9R**
Margit híd **3E**
Margit körút **2E**
Margit utca **2E**
Máriássy utca **9Z**
Mária utca **8V**
Markó utca **4F**
Márkus Emilia utca **8T**
Márton utca **9X**
Márvány utca **1J**
Mátyáshegyi út **1A**
Mátray utca **1K**
Mátyás tér **9U**
Mátyás utca **6L**
Mecset utca **2F**
Medve utca **2F**
Ménesi út **2M**
Menta utca **1L**
Mérleg utca **4H**
Mester utca **8X**
Mészáros utca **1K**
Mészöly utca **4M**
Mexikói út **12P**
Mikó utca **1H**
Mikovinyi utca **1A**
Mimóza utca **11P**

Minerva utca **4M**
Molnár utca **5K**
Montevideo utca **2A**
Mosonyi utca **10T**
Mozsár utca **5G**
Muegyetem rakpart **5M**
Munkácsy Mihály utca **8P**
Munkás utca **9S**
Murányi utca **9R**
Muskotály utca **1M**
Múzeum körút **6K**
Múzeum utca **7V**
Nádasdy utca **9Y**
Nádor utca **4H**
Nagy Diófa utca **7T**
Nagy Fuvaros utca **9U**
Nagy Ignác utca **4F**
Nagymező utca **5G**
Nagyszombat utca **2A**
Nagytemplom utca **9W**
Nagyvárad tér **11X**
Naphegy tér **2K**
Naphegy utca **2J**
Nap utca **8V**
Nedecvár utca **1M**
Nefelejcs utca **9Y**
Német utca **8U**
Népfürdo utca **5A**
Népszínház utca **9T**
Neumann János utca **7Z**
Nyár utca **7T**
Nyárs utca **1K**
Nyáry Pál utca **5K**
Október 6 utca **4H**
Olof Palme sétány **10P**
Orczy tér **11V**
Orczy út **11W**
Orgona utca **1D**
Orlay utca **4M**
Orom utca **3M**
Országház utca **1G**
Ör utca **9U**
Orvos utca **2J**
Ostrom utca **1F**
Osvát utca **8T**
Ó utca **5G**
Palánta utca **1C**
Palatinus utca **2C**
Pala utca **2H**
Pálma utca **11P**
Palota utca **2J**
Pál utca **8V**
Pálya utca **1J**
Pannónia utca **5C**
Papanövelde utca **5K**

Pápay István utca **8Y**
Párizsi utca **5J**
Párkány utca **5B**
Paulay Ede utca **5H**
Pauler utca **2J**
Páva utca **8X**
Pázmány Péter sétány **7Y**
Péceli utca **12Z**
Pesti alsó rakpart **3G**
Peterdy utca **9R**
Péterfy Sándor utca **9S**
Petőfi híd **7X**
Petőfi Sándor utca **5J**
Pilvax köz **5J**
Pipacs utca **4M**
Pipa utca **3L**
Podmaniczky utca **8P**
Ponty utca **3H**
Pozsonyi út **4E**
Práter utca **9X**
Puskin utca **6J**
Pusztaszeri út **1B**
Ráday utca **7V**
Radnóti Miklós utca **4E**
Rákóczi út **9T**
Rákospalotai határút **1E**
Raoul Wallenberg utca **4E**
Reáltanoda utca **5K**
Régiposta utca **4J**
Reguly Antal utca **11W**
Retek utca **1F**
Révay utca **5H**
Révész utca **5B**
Reviczky utca **7V**
Rezeda utca **4M**
Rezső utca **11X**
Rigó utca **8V**
Rippi Rónai utca **8P**
Róka utca **3J**
Rökk Szikárd utca **8U**
Rómer Flóris utca **1D**
Róna utca **12N**
Ronyva utca **5C**
Roosevelt tér **4H**
Rottenbiller utca **9R**
Rozgonyi utca **11W**
Rózsák tere **9S**
Rózsa utca **8R**
Rumbach Sebestyén utca **5J**
Sajó utca **10R**
Salétrom utca **8U**
Salgótarjáni utca **12U**
Sánc utca **2L**
Sárkány utca **11W**
Sarló utca **2J**
Sarolta utca **2C**

Sas utca **4H**
Schweidel utca **1L**
Semmelweis utca **5J**
Semsey Andor utca **12R**
Seregély utca **2B**
Serleg utca **2M**
Sip utca **6J**
Sobieski János utca **9X**
Sóház utca **5L**
Somlay Artúr sétány **8Y**
Somlói út **3M**
Somogyi Béla utca **8T**
Sörház utca **5K**
Soroksári útak **8Y**
Só utca **5L**
Stáhly utca **8U**
Stefánia út **11Q**
Steindl Imre utca **4G**
Stollár Béla utca **4F**
Süllő utca **6A**
Szabadság híd **5L**
Szabadság tér **4G**
Szabadsajtó út **4K**
Szabó Ilonka utca **1G**
Szabó József köz **12R**
Szabó József utca **11R**
Szabolcs utca **8P**
Szalag utca **2H**
Szalay utca **4F**
Számadó utca **2L**
Szász K utca **2F**

Százház utca **10S**
Széchenyi lánchíd **3H**
Széchenyi rakpart **4F**
Széchenyi utca **4G**
Székely Bertalan utca **8P**
Székely Mihály utca **5H**
Szemere utca **4F**
Szemlőhegy utca **1D**
Széna tér **1F**
Szende Pál utca **4J**
Szent Benedek utca **8Y**
Szent Gellért rakpart **4L**
Szent György utca **2H**
Szent István körút **4E**
Szent István tér **4H**
Szentkirályi utca **7U**
Szépvölgyi út **1A**
Szerb utca **5K**
Szerémi rakpart utca **10U**
Szeréna út **1B**
Szerk utca **12Z**
Szigony utca **9V**
Szilágyi utca **9T**
Színház utca **2H**
Szinva utca **10R**
Szinyei Merse utca **7Q**
Szirom utca **3L**
Szirtes út **3L**
Szív utca **8R**
Szobi utca **5F**

Szófia utca **7R**
Szondi utca **8P**
Szőnyi út **11N**
Szövetség utca **8S**
Szüret utca **2M**
Szűz utca **9V**
Táltos utca **1K**
Tárnok utca **2H**
Társ utca **1L**
Tátra utca **4E**
Tavaszmező utca **9V**
Teleki László tér **10U**
Telepi utca **10X**
Teréz körút **5F**
Thaly Kálmán utca **9X**
Thököly út **11R**
Thurzó utca **5D**
Tibor utca **2K**
Tigris utca **2K**
Tinódi utca **8X**
Tisza utca **5B**
Toldy Ferenc utca **2G**
Tolnai Lajos utca **9U**
Tömő utca **9W**
Tompa utca **8W**
Török Pál utca **6L**
Török utca **2E**
Tóth Árpád sétány **1H**
Tóth Kálmán utca **8Y**
Trefort utca **7U**
Turbán utca **2D**
Tutaj utca **5C**
Tüzér utca **7N**

Tűzoltó utca **8W**
Újlaki rakpart **3D**
Újpesti rakpart **4E**
Üllői út **9W**
Úri utca **2H**
Ürömi utca **2B**
Üstökös utca **2D**
Uszály utca **3B**
Uzsoki utca **12N**
Váci út **6D**
Váci utca **4J**
Vadász utca **5G**
Vágány utca **9N**
Vágóhíd utca **9Z**
Vág utca **5C**
Vajdahunyad utca **8W**
Vajda Péter utca **11W**
Vámház körút **5L**
Vám utca **2G**
Váralja utca **2J**
Varannó utca **10N**
Várfok utca **1G**
Várkert rakpart **3J**
Vármegye utca **5J**
Városház utca **5J**
Városligeti fasor **8R**
Városligeti körút **10P**
Varsányi Irén utca **1F**
Vásár utca **8U**
Vaskapu utca **8X**
Vas utca **7U**
Vay Ádám utca **9U**
Vécsei utca **4G**
Vendel utca **9X**

Veres Pálné utca **5K**
Vérhalom utca **2D**
Vérmező út **1G**
Veronika utca **2D**
Verseny utca **10S**
Vértanúk tere **4G**
Véső utca **6B**
Victor Hugo utca **5D**
Vigadó tér **4J**
Víg utca **8U**
Vigyázó Ferenc utca **4H**
Villám utca **12X**
Villányi út **2M**
Viola utca **9X**
Visegrádi utca **5D**
Visi Imre utca **11V**
Vitéz Nagy utca **2F**
Viza utca **5A**
Vörösmarty tér **4J**
Vörösmarty utca **8R**
Weiner Leó utca **5G**
Wesselényi utca **8S**
Zenta utca **4M**
Zichy Géza utca **11Q**
Zichy Jenő utca **5G**
Zichy Mihály út **11P**
Zivatar utca **1E**
Zoltán utca **4G**
Zrínyi utca **4H**
Zsigmond köz **2D**
Zsigmond tér **2C**
Zsilip utca **6A**
Zsil utca **6M**

Acknowledgements

The Automobile Association wishes to thank the following photographers, companies and picture libraries for their assistance in the preparation of this book.

Abbreviations for the picture credits are as follows – (t) top; (b) bottom; (l) left; (r) right; (c) centre; (AA) AA World Travel Library.

4l Parliament over the Danube, AA/G Wrona; **4c** Tram 2, AA/J Smith; **4r** View from Castle Hill, AA/J Smith; **5l** Rudas Baths and Gellert Hill, AA/J Smith; **5c** Széchenyi Chain Bridge, AA/J Smith; **5r** Cathedral, Esztergom, AA/K Paterson; **6/7** Parliament over the Danube, AA/G Wrona; **8/9** Gresham Palace, AA/P Wilson; **10c** Korzo promenade, AA/J Smith; **10b** Hilton Hotel Lobby, AA/P Wilson; **10/11b** Basilica, Eger, AA/P Wilson; **10/11b** View of the Danube, AA/P Wilson; **11** Eugene of Savoy Statue, AA/J Smith; **12c** Jokai bean soup, Karolyi restaurant. AA/J Smith; **12b** Paprika, AA/J Smith; **12/13** The Central Hotel, Budapest, AA/J Smith; **13t** Nokedli at Karolyi Restaurant, AA/J Smith; **13b** Butcher's Staff, Nagycsarnok, AA/J Smith; **14** Café on Váci utca, AA/J Smith; **14/15** Tokaji Wine, AA/J Smith; **16/17** Shops on Váci utca, AA/J Smith; **16b** Fisherman's Bastion, AA/J Smith; **17c** Széchenyi Chain Bridge and Buda Royal Palace at night, AA/J Smith; **17b** Vörösmarty ter, drinkers, AA/J Smith; **18** Margaret Island, Water Tower, AA/J Smith; **19t** Rudas Baths, AA/K Paterson; **19b** Budapest Royal Palace, AA/K Paterson; **20/21** Tram 2, AA/J Smith; **25** Folk Music performance, AA/K Paterson; **27** Cogwheels Railway Terminus, AA/J Smith; **34/35** View from Castle Hill, AA/J Smith; **36** Hungarian National Gallery, AA/K Paterson; **36/37** Buda Royal Palace, AA/J Smith; **38/39** Gellert Hill, view over the Danube, AA/K Paterson; **39** Gellert Hill and the Liberation Monument, AA/J Smith; **40/41** Fisherman's Bastion, AA/P Wilson; **41** Statue, Fisherman's Bastion, AA/J Smith; **42/43** State Opera House, AA/J Smith; **43** Old-fashioned State Opera sign, AA/J Smith; **44** Margaret Island Gardens, AA/J Smith; **45** View from Fisherman's Bastion over Margaret Island, AA/J Smith; **46** Matthias Church and Fisherman's Bastion, AA/J Smith; **47** Matthias Church, AA/J Smith; **48/49** Parliament and the Chain Bridge at dusk, AA/J Smith; **49** Parliament detail, AA/J Smith; **50/51** St Stephen's Basilica, AA/K Paterson; **50** Statues on St Stephen's Basilica, AA/J Smith; **51** Bell Tower, St

Stephen's Basilica, AA/J Smith; **52** Painting in the Museum of Fine Arts, AA/K Paterson; **52/53** Museum of Fine Arts, AA/J Smith; **54** Trabant Hill, view to Castle Hill, AA/K Paterson; **54/55** View to Castle Hill and the Danube, AA/J Smith; **56/57** Rudas Baths and Gellert Hill, AA/J Smith; **58/59** Cafe Kör, Travel Division Images/Alamy; **60/61** Boat trip along the River Danube, AA/K Paterson; **63** Buda Castle Funicular, AA/E Meacher; **64** War Memorial, Andrássy út, AA/P Wilson; **65** Statue of Sandor Petofi, on Petofi Sandor Street, AA/K Paterson; **66/67** Rudas Baths, AA/K Paterson; **68/69** View from Citadel over Pest, AA/J Smith; **70** Former Royal Post Office Savings Bank, AA/J Smith; **72/73** Széchenyi Chain Bridge, AA/J Smith; **75** National Széchenyi Library, AA/J Smith; **76** Statue at Vienna Gate, AA/J Smith; **76/77** Waxwork exhibition, underground labyrinth, AA/K Paterson; **78/79** Magyar Nemzeti Galeria, AA/J Smith; **81** Statue of Eugene of Savoy, AA/J Smith; **82** Church of Mary Magdalene, AA/K Paterson; **83** Orszaghaz utca, AA/J Smith; **84/85** Széchenyi Chain Bridge and Danube, AA/J Smith; **86/87** Holy Trinity Column, AA/J Smith; **88** Uri utca, AA/K Paterson; **89** Castle Theatre, AA/J Smith; **90/91** Disz ter on Castle Hill, AA/J Smith; **92/93** Király Baths, AA/J Smith; **93** Church of St Anne, AA/K Paterson; **94** Aquincum, AA/K Paterson; **94/95** Aquincum, AA/K Paterson; **105** Gellert Thermal Baths, AA/P Wilson; **106/107** Gellert Hill, AA/K Paterson; **107** Gellert Hotel, AA/P Wilson; **108** The rebuilt Liberty Bridge, AA/K Paterson; **110** Rudas Baths, AA/K Paterson; **111** Statue of Empress Elisabeth, AA/K Paterson; **115** View of Parliament and Pest, AA/K Paterson; **116** Christina Town Parish Church, AA/K Paterson; **116/117** Inner City Parish Church, AA/K Paterson; **117** Pest bank of the Danube, AA/K Paterson; **118** Budapest's Museum of Hungarian Commerce and Catering, AA K Paterson **119** Statue of Mihaly Vörösmarty at Vörösmarty ter, Peter Erik Forsberg/Alamy; **120/121** Gresham Palace, AA/K Paterson; **121** Gerbeaud Café and Pastry Shop, AA/J Smith; **122/123** Gresham Palace, AA/J Smith; **124** Ethnographical Museum, AA/K Paterson; **137** Intersection, Andrássy út and Bajcsy-Zsilinszky út, AA/J Smith; **138/139** Statue of Jokai, Jokai Ter, AA/J Smith; **139** Western Railway Station, AA/J Smith; **141** House of Terror, Beth Hall; **142** Cemetery, Orthodox Synagogue, AA/J Smith; **144/145t** Ceiling, State Opera House, AA/J Smith; **144/145b** View to Oktogon, Andrássy út; **146t** Elephant House, Zoological Garden, AA/J Smith; **146b** Art Nouveau Entrance, Zoological Gardens, AA/J Smith; **148** Millennium Monument, AA/J Smith; **159** Museum of Applied Arts, AA/K Paterson; **160/161** Hungarian National Museum, AA/J Smith; **163** Museum of Applied Arts, AA/J Smith; **164/165** National Theatre, AA/J Smith; **170/171** Cathedral, Esztergom, AA/K Paterson; **173** Buda Hills, AA/J Smith; **174/175** Statue Park, AA/J Smith; **176** Cathedral, Esztergom, AA/K Paterson; **178** Baglovestenska Orthodox Church, Szentendre, Thomas David Pinzer/Alamy; **179** The Hungarian Open Air Museum, Szentendre, Stephen Saks Photography/Alamy; **180** Visegrád, David Ball/Alamy

Every effort has been made to trace the copyright holders, and we apologise in advance for any unintentional omissions or errors. We would be happy to apply any corrections in the following edition of this publication.

Sight locator index

Arany Sas Patikamúzeum **2H**
Andrássy út **5H–9P**
Aquincum **3A** (off map)
Arpád híd **6A**
Belvárosi Plébaniatemplom **4K**
Budai Királyi Palota **3J**
Bécsi kapu **1G**
Budavári Labirintus **2H**
Budapesti Történeti Múzeum **3J**
Citadella **3L**
Dunakorzó **4J**
Erzsébet királyné szobor **4K**
Földalatti Vasúti Múzeum **5J**
Gellért Emlékmű **4K**
Gellért-hegy **4L**
Gresham Palace **4H**
Gundel Étterem **9P**
Hadtorténeti Múzeum **1G**
Halászbástya **2H**
Hercules Villa **3A** (off map)
Holokauszt Emlékközpont **8W**
Hopp Ferenc Kelet-Ázsiai Művészeti Múzeum **8Q**
Hősök tere **9P**
Hotel Gellért és Gellért Gyógyfürdő **4M**
Iparművészeti Múzeum **8W**
Kerepesi temető **11U**
Király Gyógyfürdő **2F**

Közlekedési Múzeum **11P**
Liszt Ferenc Emlekmúzeum **8R**
Ludwig Múzeum Budapest **8Z**
Magyar Állami Operaház **5G**
Magyar Kereskedelmi és Vendéglátóipari Múzeum **5H**
Magyar Királyi Posta Takarékpénztár **4G**
Magyar Nemzeti Galéria **3J**
Magyar Nemzeti Múzeum **6K**
Magyar Tudományos Akadémia **4H**
Magyar Természettudományi Múzeum **10W**
Margitsziget **4B**
Mária Magdolna-Torony **1G**
Mátyás-kút **3J**
Mátyás-templom **2H**
Művészetek Palotája **8Z**
Nagy zsinagóga **6J**
Nemzeti színház **8Z**
Néprajzi Múzeum **4F**
New York Kávéház **8T**
Nyugati Pályaudvar **5F**
Öntödei Múzeum **2F**
Országház **3F**
Országház utca **1G**
Országos Széchényi Könyvtár **3J**
Postamúzeum **5H**

Régi Budai Városháza **2H**
Roth Miksa Emlékház **9S**
Rudas Gyógyfürdő **4K**
Savoyai Jenő szobor **3J**
Semmelweis Orvostörténeti Múzeum **3K**
Sikló **3J**
Szabadság híd **5L**
Szabadság szobor **4L**
Szabadság tér **4G**
Szarvas-ház **3K**
Széchenyi lánchíd **3H**
Szentháromság szobor **2H**
Szent Anna templom **3F**
Szent István Bazilika **5H**
Szépművészeti Múzeum **9P**
Sziklatemplom **4L**
Terror Háza **7R**
Telefónia Múzeum **1G**
Úri utca **2H**
Váci utca **4J**
Vár-hegy **1H**
Városliget **10P**
Várszinház **2H**
Vásárcsarnok **5L**
Vörösmarty tér **4J**
Zeneakadémia **7S**

Dear Reader

Your comments, opinions and recommendations are very important to us. Please help us to improve our travel guides by taking a few minutes to complete this simple questionnaire.

You do not need a stamp (unless posted outside the UK). If you do not want to cut this page from your guide, then photocopy it or write your answers on a plain sheet of paper.

Send to: **The Editor, AA World Travel Guides,**
FREEPOST SCE 4598, Basingstoke RG21 4GY.

Your recommendations...

We always encourage readers' recommendations for restaurants, nightlife or shopping – if your recommendation is used in the next edition of the guide, we will send you a **FREE AA Guide** of your choice from this series. Please state below the establishment name, location and your reasons for recommending it.

_____
_____
_____
_____
_____

Please send me **AA Guide** _____

About this guide...
Which title did you buy?
AA _____
Where did you buy it? _____
When? m m / y y
Why did you choose this guide? _____
_____
_____
_____

Did this guide meet your expectations?

Exceeded ☐ Met all ☐ Met most ☐ Fell below ☐

Were there any aspects of this guide that you particularly liked? _____
_____
_____

continued on next page...

Is there anything we could have done better? _____

_____

_____

About you...

Name (*Mr/Mrs/Ms*) _____

Address _____

_____ Postcode _____

Daytime tel nos _____

Email _____

Please only give us your mobile phone num
other products and services from the AA an

Which age group are you in?
Under 25 ☐ 25–34 ☐ 35–44 ☐ 4

How many trips do you make a year?
Less than one ☐ One ☐ Two ☐

Are you an AA member? Yes ☐ No ☐

About your trip...

When did you book? m m / ϒ ϒ   W

How long did you stay? _____

Was it for business or leisure? _____

Did you buy any other travel guides for yo

If yes, which ones? _____

_____

_____

Thank you for taking the time to complete
possible, and remember, you do not need

AA Travel Insurance call 080

A & H

3013020127521 0

ESSEX COUNTY COUNCIL

S40245S